בס"ד

Beacons on the Talmud's Sea

ANALYSES OF PASSAGES FROM THE TALMUD AND ISSUES IN HALACHAH

Adapted from the Works of
the Lubavitcher Rebbe
Rabbi Menachem M. Schneerson

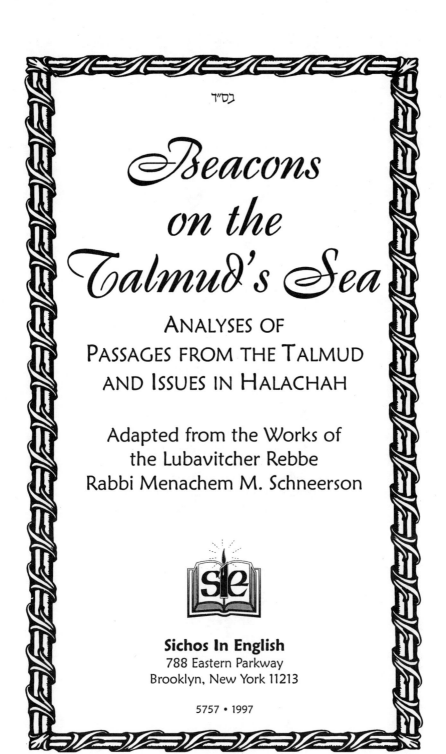

Sichos In English
788 Eastern Parkway
Brooklyn, New York 11213

5757 • 1997

BEACONS ON THE TALMUD'S SEA

Published and Copyrighted by
SICHOS IN ENGLISH
788 Eastern Parkway • Brooklyn, N.Y. 11213
Tel. (718) 778-5436

ISBN 1-8814-0026-3

5757 • 1997

TABLE OF CONTENTS

PUBLISHER'S FOREWORD

ONE TORAH As leaders of the chassidic and Lithuanian communities respectively, the third Lubavitcher Rebbe, known as the *Tzemach Tzedek,* and R. Yitzchak of Volozhin, worked together on many projects for the welfare of the Jewish community in nineteenth-century Russia. A by-product of the spirit of cooperation they shared was an increased mood of communication and respect between chassidim and *misnagdim*, bridging the gaps that had previously separated these two camps.

People were wont to say: "Through this relationship, the *misnagdim* learned that the *tzaddikim* revered by the chassidim were giants of Torah, and the chassidim were able to appreciate that the Torah luminaries held in awe by the *misnagdim* were also *tzaddikim.*"

The intellectual underpinnings for such an understanding lie at the heart of the chassidic approach to Torah study. For *Chassidus* does not view Torah study and *avodas HaShem,* divine service, as two separate disciplines, but as two elements of a unified thrust to personal refinement and the fulfillment of G-d's will. More particularly, *nigleh,* the revealed teachings of Torah law, and *pnimiyus haTorah,* the mystical secrets of Torah, should not be seen as two separate courses of study, but as the body and the soul of the same Torah.

Hence, as the Rebbe Rashab states in *Kuntreis Etz Chayim* (when giving directives for the students of *Yeshivas Tomchei Temimim,* the Central Lubavitcher *Yeshivah*): "It should be evident that a student who studies *pnimiyus haTorah* has studied *nigleh.* And it should be evident that a student who studies *nigleh* has studied *pnimiyus haTorah.*"

If these concepts hold true regarding the Torah study of chassidim, they surely apply with regard to the Rebbeim, the exemplars to whom we look for guidance and direction.

It is not the place of a chassid to rank the Rebbeim, or even to describe them with superlatives. For to apply any description — even a superlative — to a person, implies that one is on a level at which one can comprehend and appreciate the qualities that the other possesses.

This said, it goes without saying that the Rebbeim of *Chabad,* beginning with the Alter Rebbe and including the Rebbe of our generation, were all giants of soul and giants of scholarship, that their stature was reflected in their mastery of both *nigleh* and *pnimiyus haTorah,* and that because of their mastery of *pnimiyus haTorah,* their approach to *nigleh* was distinctive and unique.

TASTE AND SEE Significantly, this area has not been given adequate focus in the English language. None of the works in *nigleh* of the previous *Chabad* Rebbeim have ever been translated into English. And although many of the subjects in *Likkutei Sichos* and the Rebbe's other published works include explanations in the realm of *nigleh*, relatively few of them have been presented in a language other than the original Yiddish or *Lashon HaKodesh*.

Perhaps the reason for this lack is the uniqueness mentioned above. The Rebbe's explanation of an issue in *nigleh* involves a breadth and depth that can best be perceived and appreciated by a person who has the skills to study the subject matter in its original.

For this reason, we had to grapple with certain misgivings while preparing the text. Unquestionably, in the process of translation and adaptation, some of the nuances of the Rebbe's style had to be sacrificed. Nevertheless, we considered the alternative — leaving the subject matter reserved only for those who can comprehend the original — far less desirable, for that would leave a multitude of people for whom this dimension of the Rebbe's thoughts would remain inaccessible.

And so, to give our readers the opportunity to taste the Rebbe's singular approach to this body of knowledge, we decided to produce a "sampler": a book which reflects the Rebbe's treatment of a variety of different subjects in *nigleh*.

Because of the factors mentioned above, the essays themselves — with the exception of the essay entitled "Of Eternal Life" — are also "samplers": that is, they are adaptations, not translations. In the original texts, there is a detailed intellectual give and take which, though lending richness to one's comprehension of the ideas, is difficult to render into English, and which might blur the focus of a reader unfamiliar with this style of thought. Hence, in many instances, we chose to telescope an intricate discussion into a conceptual outline that preserves the insight of the original ideas while trying to avoid arduous complexity.

AREAS OF FOCUS   The essays are arranged in four sections:
a) Distinctive Stances in the *Talmud:* Three essays which show how a Sage or a school of Sages follow a distinctive pattern of reasoning *(azlinan leshitaso)* which sheds light on their characteristic approaches to a variety of seemingly unrelated matters.

b) Holidays in Torah Law: A treatment of the halachic dimension of the holidays and communal fasts.[1]

c) Unlocking the *Aggadah:* The *Aggadah* teaches the homiletical and ethical dimensions of Torah thought. These four essays demonstrate how the insights of *Chassidus* can imbue this realm of knowledge with a new and penetrating light.

d) Issues in the *Halachah:* In-depth analyses of particular halachic issues or Talmudic passages.

As the term "sampler" implies, the subjects were chosen because they were felt to be indicative of the Rebbe's style of teaching, or because they reflected subjects which the Rebbe would frequently emphasize.

COMBINED EFFORTS   When listing "the distinctions by which the Torah is acquired," *Pirkei Avos* mentions[2] "close association with colleagues and sharp discussions with students." For to step beyond one's own subjectivity and objectively appreciate the truth of the Torah, the interplay of many different

---

1. Fasts are included in this category because, as explained in the essay entitled "An End to Fasting," they are holidays *in potentia*. In the Era of the Redemption, the positive dimension of these dates will be revealed and they will be celebrated as holidays (cf. *Zechariah* 8:19).

2. 6:6.

approaches is necessary. Every individual's understanding is sharpened by exposure to other people's way of thought.

Accordingly, this text fuses the efforts of many diverse contributors. In particular: Rabbi Eliyahu Touger, who was responsible for the translation; Rabbi Aharon Leib Raskin, who annotated the sources and checked the authenticity of the translation; Yosef Yitzchok Turner, who attended to the layout and typography; and Rabbi Yonah Avtzon, Director of Sichos In English, who supervised every phase of the project's development.

SPREADING	Once a *yeshivah* student approached
THE	the Rebbe with a dilemma. Although
WELLSPRINGS	his personal preference and talents

lay in the study of *nigleh*, he nevertheless felt compelled to devote himself to the study of *Chassidus* because, as the Rebbe would frequently quote,[3] it is spreading the wellsprings of the Baal Shem Tov's teachings that will hasten the coming of *Mashiach*.

While not discouraging his study of *Chassidus*, the Rebbe answered the youth that the study of *nigleh*, particularly as it is illuminated by the teachings of the Rebbeim, is also considered "spreading the wellsprings outward."

It is thus appropriate that many of the essays conclude with an emphasis on the coming of the Redemption. Indeed, in a larger sense, all of our spiritual endeavors should be directed to this goal.

May the study of the Rebbe's teachings encourage us all to assume our part in shouldering the mission of spiri-

---

3. See the letter of the Baal Shem Tov to his brother-in-law, R. Gershon Kitover, at the beginning of *Keser Shem Tov*.

tual purpose which the Rebbe taught. And may this in turn lead to *manifest* good and blessing, including the ultimate blessing — the coming of the Redemption, when we will merit the teachings of *Mashiach,* "the new [dimensions of the] Torah" which will "emerge from Me."[4]

Sichos In English

Pesach Sheni, 5757

---

4.   Cf. *Yeshayahu* 51:4; *Vayikra Rabbah* 13:3.

DISTINCTIVE STANCES IN THE *TALMUD*

"LOVE AND TRUTH CONVERGE":

AN ANALYSIS OF THE DIFFERENT CHARACTERISTICS OF THE SCHOOLS OF HILLEL AND SHAMMAI

Adapted from *Likkutei Sichos,* Vol. II, p. 321ff.; Vol. IV, p.
1121; Vol. VI, p. 69ff.; Vol. XVI, p. 312ff.; Vol. XXI,
p.115ff.; Vol. XXII, p. 47ff.; *Toras Menachem Hadranim,* p.
375; *Sefer HaSichos 5751,* Vol. II, p. 566ff.; *Sichos
Shabbos Parshas Bamidbar, 5734*

OUT OF THE ONE, MANY   The *Talmud*[1] states:

It is written:[2] "The words of the wise are like spurs, and like nails well driven in are [the words of] the masters of collections; they are given from one Shepherd...."

"The masters of collections" — these are the students of the Sages who sit in different groups and

---

1.   *Chagigah* 3b.
2.   *Koheles* 12:11.

3

engage themselves in Torah study. Some will rule [that an object is] impure, and others will rule [that it is pure]. Some will declare [an object] unacceptable, and others will declare [it] acceptable.

If a person will ask: "How is it possible for me to study the Torah under such circumstances?" — the verse continues: "[These words] were given from one Shepherd." One G-d gave them, and one master[3] communicated them.

The concept of variety and difference within the Torah is also reflected in our Sages' account of the very source of our Torah heritage, the communication of the Oral Law to Moshe on Mount Sinai. Our Sages relate:[4]

On each law, [the Holy One, blessed be He,] would teach [Moshe] 49 perspectives [leading to the ruling that an object is] impure, and 49 perspectives [leading to the ruling that it is] pure.

Moshe exclaimed: "Master of the World, when will I be able to reach the clarification of these matters?"

The Holy One, blessed be He, told him: "Follow the majority.[5] If the majority rules that it is impure, it is impure. If the majority rules that it is pure, it is pure."

The Torah is spiritual truth, existing on a level above worldly existence.[6] And yet, it is not intended to remain

3. Moshe (Rashi's commentary, loc. cit.).
4. Jerusalem Talmud, Sanhedrin 4:2; Midrash Tehillim 12:7.
5. See Shmos 23:2 and commentaries; Rambam, Mishneh Torah, Hilchos Sanhedrin 8:1.
6. See Bereishis Rabbah 8:2, et al., which states that the Torah predated the world.

on that lofty plane, but rather to descend and relate to our experience in this world. Nevertheless, because it is lofty and abstract, this process of descent leads to a variety of conceptions. As pure light takes on many colors when filtered through a prism, so too, as the Torah's truth comes in contact with material existence, different perspectives arise. For the same principle can motivate two opposite conclusions.

To cite an example: Before the Flood,[7] "G-d saw that... every impulse of the thoughts of [man's] heart was only for evil... And G-d said, 'I will obliterate mankind.'" After the Flood, when Noach offered sacrifices, G-d said:[8] "I will not continue to curse the earth, because of man, for the impulse of man's heart is evil." One factor, the *yetzer hara's* constant temptation of man, serves as the rationale calling for both the Flood, and for G-d's promise never to repeat such disasters.

In a similar way, each of the *Tannaim* and *Amoraim* would view the Torah's laws as they exist in their spiritual source. Nevertheless, to determine a ruling regarding a particular situation, a Sage would have to sift through the relevant legal principles and apply them to the circumstances at hand. And for every Sage, this process of analysis was guided by the thrust of his spiritual personality. As his awareness of the spiritual motivation for the law became intertwined with his appreciation of the germane factors, the Sage's decision would shape and form.

Often the decisions reached by the Sages would differ, for the processes of determination that characterized one would vary from that of the other. And with regard to

---

7.   *Bereishis* 6:5-6.
8.   *Ibid.*, 8:21.

these differences, it is said:[9] "These and these are the words of the living G-d." For the truth of Torah contains the potential for manifold expressions. This dictum was applied, however, only in the realm of theory. With regard to practice, the Torah tradition has always sought uniformity,[10] and when differences of opinion arise, the *halachah* is established according to the majority.[11]

INTROSPECTION AND OUTREACH The above concepts apply not only with regard to the Oral Tradition as a whole, but with regard to particular phases in its transmission. For example, Hillel and Shammai received the Oral Tradition from the same masters, Shemayah and Avtalyon.[12] Nevertheless, they — and to a greater extent, their students — developed these thoughts in different directions. And thus throughout the *Talmud,* we find differences of opinion between the School of Shammai and the School of Hillel.

In most instances, the School of Hillel would rule more leniently and the School of Shammai more stringently. What was the source for these differences?[13] Hillel's approach was characterized by the attribute of *Chesed,* kindness, while Shammai's was distinguished by the attribute of *Gevurah,* might, which tends toward severity.

---

9. *Eruvin* 13b.
10. See *Ta'amei HaMitzvos* (of the *AriZal*), *Parshas Ki Seitzei,* which states that "every (Sage) would relate the truth as perceived by his spiritual rung. *Halachah* is determined according to the nature of the time."
11. The determination of Torah law also involves a respect for precedents. A later court cannot change a ruling adopted by a previous court unless "it is greater than its predecessors in wisdom and in the number of adherents it has" (*Rambam, Mishneh Torah, Hilchos Mamrim* 2:1-2).
12. *Avos* 1:12; See *Hemshech 5672,* Vol. I, p. 20ff.
13. *Zohar,* Vol. III, p. 245a, 281a; *Tanya, Iggeres HaKodesh,* Epistle 13.

Gevurah has an inward thrust, as reflected in our Sages' statement:[14] "Who is a *gibbor* (mighty man)? One who conquers his inclination." And according to the *Kabbalah,* the attribute of *Gevurah* is identified with *din,* judgment. A person who tends toward *Gevurah* has unalterable standards of truth to which he personally endeavors to conform and which he desires to see reflected in the world at large. This is implied by the name Shammai, which relates to the Hebrew phrase:[15] *hasham orchosov,* "He evaluates his ways,"[16] i.e., he is constantly subjecting his conduct to rigorous introspection.

Chesed, by contrast, reflects an outward orientation. Others are one's primary concern. A person motivated by *chesed* extends himself and gives, following the path Hillel outlines,[17] "Loving peace and pursuing peace; loving the created beings[18] and drawing them close to the Torah." This approach also relates to Hillel's name which is associated with the phrase *behilo neiro,*[15] "When His candle shined forth."[19] For this approach emphasizes disseminating light, with the expectation that it will effortlessly cause darkness to shrink. And as light diffuses into wider peripheries, it attracts people and motivates them to change.

"THE REST IS COMMENTARY"   These character thrusts are reflected in the classic story[20] of the

---

14. *Avos* 4:1.
15. *Likkutei Torah, Shir HaShirim,* p. 48b ff.
16. *Moed Kattan* 5a.
17. *Avos* 1:12.
18. I.e., this includes even such individuals whose only redeeming quality is that they are G-d's creations (see *Tanya,* ch. 32).
19. *Iyov* 29:3.
20. *Shabbos* 31a.

potential convert who approached Shammai and asked him to teach him the entire Torah while he stood on one foot. Shammai "drove him away with a measuring rod." When, however, the person came to Hillel with the same request, Hillel told him to stand, and taught him: "What is hateful to you, do not do to your colleague. This is the entire Torah; the rest is commentary. Go and learn."

Shammai was demanding of himself, and to the same degree, he was demanding of others. This is implied by the phrase: "he drove him away with a measuring rod." As he stood before Shammai, the potential convert did not measure up to the expectations which Shammai had of his students.

Hillel, by contrast, was willing to patiently extend himself. He appreciated the potential convert's spiritual state as Shammai had, but he also saw a possibility for growth. Therefore, he communicated a fundamental Torah concept to the potential convert on a level to which he could relate. And it had an effect; the man converted and began proceeding on the Torah's unending path of personal development.

"TO DRAW CLOSE WITH THE RIGHT HAND AND REBUFF WITH THE LEFT"

A similar pattern is reflected in the general thrust of the *halachic* rulings of these Sages and their disciples. Because Hillel's spiritual thrust was characterized by kindness, he would take a patient look at every situation, seeing whether there was a way it could serve the purpose of holiness. If he could discover such a possibility, he would rule leniently.

Shammai, by contrast, guarded the standards of holiness with meticulous rigor, and if it appeared that an object did not meet those standards, he ruled stringently. Rather than risk the possibility of spiritual decline, he forbade contact with such objects, and thus forestalled any negative repercussions.

It must, however, be emphasized that neither Hillel nor Shammai — nor any of the other Sages of the Talmud — solely followed their own personal tendencies when delivering *halachic* rulings. On the contrary, our Sages described[21] the differences of opinion between Hillel and Shammai as being maintained "for the sake of Heaven." In a desire to ascertain G-d's law, they sought to rise above their personal tendencies, and to be objective. Accordingly, Hillel would sometimes arrive at a more stringent ruling and Shammai would occasionally rule more leniently.

Nevertheless, by and large, the Sages would perceive the truth as filtered through their natural spiritual thrust. And therefore, Hillel and his students would predominantly rule more leniently, and Shammai and his students, more stringently.

TOWARDS A MORE COMPREHENSIVE UNDERSTANDING The above concepts are reflected, not only in the overall thrusts toward leniency and stringency evident in the rulings of the Schools of Shammai and Hillel, but also in theoretical constructs of a middle range, i.e., motifs that connect seemingly unrelated rulings throughout the *Talmud*. A particular difference of opinion mentioned in one source appears not as an isolated phenomenon but as part of a paradigm of a more general scope. To use the terminology

---

21. *Avos* 5:17.

employed by the *Talmud* in certain instances, *azlinan lishitoso*, "we follow his pattern of logic."

The following are several examples of such patterns: With regard to the blessing recited over the candle during the *havdalah* ceremony:[22] The School of Shammai rules that the conclusion of the blessing should be: *borei maor haeish*, praising G-d as "the Creator of the light of fire." The School of Hillel, by contrast, rules that the text of the blessing should be: *borei meorei haeish*, "the Creator of the lights of fire," employing a plural form.

We cannot say that the difference of opinion focuses on a point of actual fact: whether there are several lights in a flame or just one light, for it is obvious that there are several colors in a flame. There is no way that the School of Shammai can dispute this.[23] Instead, the difference of opinion is: which aspect of the flame is of primary concern?

To explain: When one sees a flame, one immediately sees light. Afterwards, as one looks more closely, one sees that this light is comprised of several different colors. The School of Shammai puts the emphasis on one's initial perception, while the School of Hillel, by contrast, highlights the conception that one would reach after a more patient look.

APPRECIATING A BRIDE'S BEAUTY   A similar motif is reflected in the praise which is traditionally given

---

22. *Berachos* 51b. There the *Mishnah* states the two conflicting rulings; see also the explanation in the *Gemara*, 52b.

23. Indeed, for reasons such as this, an effort is always made to explain how a difference of opinion between Sages stems, not from a point of fact which can be verified, but rather from a point of theory, so that there not be a *machlokes bimetzius*.

a bride.[24] The School of Shammai maintains that a bride should be praised according to the positive qualities which she personally possesses,[25] while the School of Hillel states that all brides should be praised as being "beautiful and gracious."

The School of Shammai asked the School of Hillel: "If a bride limps or is blind, should one praise her as being 'beautiful and gracious'? Has not the Torah told us,[26] 'Keep your distance from falsehood'?"

The School of Hillel responded: "When a person buys an inferior article in the market, should one praise it in his presence, or should one find fault with it in his presence? It appears to us that one should praise it for him." As the *Talmud* concludes, the thrust of the School of Hillel was to be considerate of others and their feelings.

The School of Hillel was not stating that one should lie and praise a bride with qualities which she did not possess. Their perspective is that every groom surely considers his bride as "beautiful and gracious." And if a person wants to make a friend feel gratified by praising his bride, the person offering the praise should be patient enough to think over the matter carefully until he appreciates the qualities which cause her groom to see her as "beautiful and gracious."

The School of Shammai, by contrast, does not require a person to make such an involved and careful analysis. A person should endeavor to make a groom feel happy, and emphasize the positive qualities which a bride possesses that are overtly obvious. One should not, however, make statements which do not appear to be true.

---

24. *Kesubbos* 16b ff.
25. See the interpretation of *Tosafos*.
26. *Shmos* 23:7.

As in the previous instance, the School of Shammai gives priority to a person's initial perception. The School of Hillel, by contrast, underscores the need for extending oneself, and taking a more involved and more detailed look at the situation at hand.

LOOKING AT THE COVER, OR AT WHAT'S INSIDE IT

A third example of this pattern can be seen in the Rogachover Gaon's interpretation[27] of the difference of opinion between the School of Shammai and the School of Hillel with regard to whether or not the covers of sacred scrolls are susceptible to the contraction of ritual impurity.[28] The School of Shammai maintains that regardless of whether the cover of a scroll is embroidered with ornamental patterns or not, the cover is susceptible to ritual impurity.

The ruling of the School of Hillel is based on the principle that it is functional articles, not ornaments, which are susceptible to ritual impurity. As such, an ordinary cover is considered as an article which serves a purpose, and therefore is susceptible to ritual impurity. The primary purpose of an embroidered cover, however, is considered its aesthetic dimension, and not the function it serves. Hence, such a cover is not susceptible to ritual impurity.

The Rogatchover Gaon explains[29] why the School of Shammai does not make a distinction between one type of

---

27. *Tzafnas Paneach Responsa* (New York), Responsum 136, cited in *Tzafnas Paneach al HaTorah, Parshas Shemini*, p. 106.
28. *Keilim* 28:4.
29. Based on the Raavad's gloss to *Toras Kohanim, Parshas Shemini*. The *Rambam*, the *Rosh*, and Rav Ovadiah of Bartenura offer different interpretations of this *Mishnah* which do not conform as closely to

cover and the other. Since at first glance, both types of covers appear the same, no differentiation is made between the rulings that apply to them. The School of Hillel, by contrast, accentuates the particular characteristics of each type of cover, and accordingly, places them in different categories. In this instance as well, the School of Hillel's approach is characterized by a patient process of distinction that focuses on the particulars, while the approach of the School of Shammai focuses on the general impression[30] that immediately arises.[31]

---

this conception of the difference in interpretation between the Schools of Shammai and Hillel.

30. The intent is not that the School of Shammai does not have the ability to discern particulars. On the contrary, our Sages *(Yevamos* 14a; *Tosafos, Eruvin* 6b) describe them as being "sharper and more astute," than the School of Hillel. Nevertheless, their powers of discernment were focused on abstracting a general conception from the particulars, and not on appreciating the particulars *per se.*

31. The same pattern is reflected in the story of the convert cited above (and in two similar narratives quoted in *Shabbos, loc. cit.*). Shammai related to the potential convert according to the general impression he initially projected, while Hillel patiently considered the full picture into which the person could blossom. Similarly, there are other examples of this pattern in the *Talmud.* The rulings cited above were intended to serve as prototypes of this conception to which other parallels can be found.

{Trans. note: Here we see a connection to Hillel's dominant trait of *Chesed* (kindness) and Shammai's traits of *Gevurah* (might) and *Din* (judgment). Following the principle *(Sanhedrin* 6b) that: "A judge [takes into consideration] only what is perceivable to his eyes," the School of Shammai would make their determination according to the factors which were obvious, and a person or object which did not meet their standards would be firmly rejected.

With patient kindness, the School of Hillel would, by contrast, consider all the factors of a situation, and contemplate the full range of realizable means of expression, and when possible, underscore the positive dimensions.}

THE POTENTIAL FOR LIGHT Another general pattern which characterizes several of the differences of opinion between the School of Shammai and the School of Hillel can be seen in their rulings regarding the order of the kindling of Chanukah lights.[32] The School of Shammai rules that on the first night, eight candles should be lit, on the second night seven, each night reducing the number. The School of Hillel, by contrast, maintains that on the first night, one candle should be lit, on the second night, two, and it is only on the last night that eight candles are lit.

What is the rationale which motivates their different rulings?[33] The School of Shammai focuses on the potential (the *ko'ach,* in *yeshivah* terminology). On the first night of Chanukah, there is a potential for eight days; every night, the potential is reduced. The School of Hillel, by contrast, focuses on the actual (the *poel,* in *yeshivah* terminology). On the first night, there is only one day of Chanukah which is actually being celebrated. Each day, another day is added, until on the eighth day, the full potential of the holiday has been expressed in actual practice. Accordingly, eight candles are lit.

---

32. *Shabbos* 21b.
33. See the explanation of parallel concepts in *Beis Otzar* by R. Yosef Engel *(Os Alef,* sec. 27; *Os Beis,* sec. 2)* and *LeOr HaHalachah* by R. Shlomo Y. Zevin. The example cited above and those to follow are not the only reflections of this pattern throughout the *Talmud,* but rather paradigms that clearly express the theme of each school.

{Trans. note: Here, too, a connection can be drawn to the attributes of *Din* (judgment) and *Chesed* (kindness). For Shammai's emphasis on the potential relates to the objective standard of *Din,* according to which every situation is judged. Hillel's emphasis on the actual reflects the tendency of *Chesed* to encourage the full manifestation of all potentials.}

| THE TIME OF THE
| REDEMPTION

To cite another example of this pattern: The School of Shammai maintains[34] that during the recitation of the *Hallel* at the Pesach *Seder,* we should recite only the first psalm, *Hallelu avdei HaShem,* before partaking of the meal. The School of Hillel, by contrast, maintains that we should also recite the second psalm, *B'tzeis Yisrael MiMitzrayim,* "When Israel left Egypt," before partaking of the meal.

In explanation of their difference of opinion, the *Jerusalem Talmud* relates:[35]

> The School of Shammai said to them: "Why mention the exodus from Egypt [at this point]? Did the children of Israel leave Egypt [before partaking of the Paschal sacrifice]?"

> The School of Hillel responded to them: "Even if you were to wait until the rooster's crow, you would not reach halfway to [the time of] the Redemption.... For they did not leave until noon."

The School of Shammai maintains that the potential for the Redemption came with the eating of the Paschal sacrifice. Hence, after partaking of that sacrifice, it is fit to recite "When Israel left Egypt." The School of Hillel, by contrast, maintains that since the actual exodus did not take place until midday, there is no point in delaying recitation of the psalm, and it should be recited even before partaking of the Paschal sacrifice.

---

34. *Pesachim* 116b.
35. *Pesachim* 10:5; *Tosefta, Pesachim* 10:6.

THE CONCLUSION OF THE TALMUD   Another example of this difference in approach can be seen in the laws which conclude the entire *Talmud*. The *Mishnah*[36] states:

> Fish: when do they become susceptible to the contraction of ritual impurity?[37] The School of Shammai states: "When they are caught." The School of Hillel states: "When they die.". ...

> Honeycombs: when do they become considered as liquids [which make other foods] fit to contract ritual impurity?[38] The School of Shammai states: "When one thinks about [removing the honey]."[39] The School of Hillel states: "When one crushes [the honeycomb]."

Since fish will die shortly after they are caught and removed from the water, the School of Shammai maintains that they are susceptible to ritual impurity as soon as they are caught. From this time onward, there is the potential to use them as food, and this makes them susceptible to impurity. The School of Hillel, by contrast, maintains that until the fish actually die, they are not considered as food, nor are they susceptible to impurity.

---

36. *Uktzin* 3:9, 11.

37. A living being never contracts ritual impurity, while foods do. The question is: At which point are fish considered to have become food?

38. Produce is not susceptible to ritual impurity until it comes in contact with one of seven liquids: water, wine, oil, milk, honey, dew, or blood. The question in this *mishnah* is: When is the honey in the honeycombs considered as a liquid?

39. This version is found in the texts of Rabbeinu Hai, Rabbeinu Shimon, Rabbeinu Asher, and others. The standard printed texts, the *Aruch*, the *Rambam*, and others, follow a different version which states: "When one creates smoke" for the purpose of driving away the bees (the *Aruch*) or heating the honeycomb to remove the honey (the *Rambam*).

Similarly, with regard to honeycombs, since the potential exists for the honey to be removed from them, the School of Shammai maintains that as soon as one decides to take this step,[40] the honey is considered as a liquid. The School of Hillel, by contrast, maintains that until one actually crushes the honeycomb to remove the honey, it is not considered as a liquid.

HEAVEN OR EARTH   The fact that this difference of opinion between the School of Shammai and the School of Hillel was chosen as the subject for the final laws to be discussed by the *Mishnah*[41] indicates that it is of general importance. And indeed, we find the same thrust motivating two passages which quote differences of opinion between the Schools of Hillel and Shammai that relate to the purpose of the creation and the purpose of man.

With regard to the purpose of creation, it is stated:[42]

> The School of Shammai says: "The heavens were created first, and then the earth...." The School of Hillel says: "The earth was created first, and then the heavens."

The Alter Rebbe explains[43] that with regard to the order of creation, the heavens — the spiritual worlds — were created before this material world, and indeed, it is the spiritual realms that convey the life energy which

---

40. Or according to the other versions of the *mishnah,* as soon as one begins the preliminary activities for this purpose.

41. The *Mishnah* concludes with a teaching describing the reward the righteous will receive in the Era of the Redemption. This teaching is not directly connected to the *halachic* concepts that precede it, but is included so that the *Mishnah* will conclude with a positive theme.

42. *Chagigah* 12a; *Bereishis Rabbah* 1:15.

43. *Torah Or,* at the beginning of *Parshas Vayigash.*

brings this world into being. Nevertheless, the purpose of creation is our material world; to borrow a phrase,[44] "Last in deed, first in [G-d's] thought." Or, to refer to an analogy, when one constructs a building, it is the ultimate product which reflects the builder's original intent.

This resolution requires further explanation, for it implies that the School of Hillel and the School of Shammai are speaking about different aspects of the creation — the School of Shammai, the order of creation, and the School of Hillel, the intent — and there is no difference of opinion between them. The form of the quotation: "The School of Shammai says:.... The School of Hillel says:....", however, implies that they do not accept each other's positions.

Upon what does their difference of opinion revolve? Not on their opinions with regard to chronological precedence, but rather upon their conception of what is of primary importance. According to the School of Hillel, the earth is of paramount importance — it is in this material realm that G-d's intent for creation is expressed. The School of Shammai maintains that, although G-d's intent is expressed in this material world, the intent is first manifest in the heavens — in spiritual reality. And the entire thrust of our Divine service is to elevate material existence to the point that it can reflect this spiritual reality. The School of Hillel is thus putting the emphasis on the actual expression of the intent for creation (the *poel*), while the School of Shammai is highlighting the spiritual truths that enable this intent to be expressed (the *ko'ach*).[45]

---

44. The *Lecha Dodi* hymn, *Shabbos* liturgy, *Siddur Tehillat HaShem*, p. 132.
45. Here also we see a connection to the attributes of *Chesed* and *Gevurah*. For *Gevurah* is characterized by *he'elem*, concealment, which relates to the *ko'ach*, for, by definition, a potential is not overtly evident. *Chesed*, by contrast, is characterized by *gilui*, revelation. This relates to the

This concept also enables us to understand why in all matters, the School of Shammai places the emphasis on the *ko'ach*. Since they conceive of the purpose of creation as elevating the material to the spiritual, it is the spiritual conception — the *ko'ach* — which receives priority. The School of Hillel, by contrast, conceives of the intent of creation as having spiritual truth made manifest in our material world. Hence, their emphasis is on actual expression — the *poel*.[46]

TO BE, OR NOT TO BE   Similar concepts apply with regard to the purpose of the creation of man. Our Sages state:[47]

For two and a half years, there was a difference of opinion between the School of Shammai and the School of Hillel. These (the School of Shammai)[48] would say: "It is better for a person not to have been born than to have been born." And these (the

---

poel, for it is the actual expression that brings a subject into revelation.

46. This also reflects how the thrusts of Divine service expressed by these two schools are outgrowths of the attributes of *Chesed* and *Gevurah*. The attribute of *Gevurah* is characterized by a movement towards ascent in Divine service, elevating and refining the material realm so that it reflects the spiritual. Conversely, the attribute of *Chesed* is characterized by a downward thrust in Divine service, bringing the spiritual into manifestation within our material world.

47. *Eruvin* 13b.

48. The *Talmud* states that this passage reflects a difference of opinion between the School of Shammai and the School of Hillel, but does not state explicitly which school made which statement. Nevertheless, since throughout the *Talmud,* the opinion of the School of Shammai is cited before the School of Hillel, it is likely that this pattern is followed in this instance as well. See the gloss of the *Ritva* to *Eruvin, loc. cit.,* and the gloss of the *Radbaz* to *Rambam, Mishneh Torah, Hilchos Maaser Sheni* 6:3.

School of Hillel) would say: "It is better for a person
to have been born than not to have been born."

The School of Shammai, who highlights the potential,
says that it is better for a person not to have been born,
because the potential for personal fulfillment already
exists in the spiritual realms. A person's existence in this
world is — at its best — merely an expression of his
spiritual potential. This is essential to fulfill G-d's purpose
in creation, but *"for a person,"* i.e., from his own individual standpoint, it is preferable that he not have been
created.

The School of Hillel, who focuses on actual expression, maintains that it is through the descent into this
world that a soul reaches the heights of fulfillment. For
the observance of the Torah and its *mitzvos* on this material plane lifts a person to a level above its previous rung
in the spiritual realms. Therefore, it is preferable for the
person to have been born.

This leads to a further point. Since the School of
Shammai puts the emphasis on G-d's desire, and not
man's, man's Divine service is characterized by self-nullification, the negation of his own will. As such, it is "better
for a person not to have been born."

The School of Hillel, by contrast, sees man's fulfillment as a personal goal. G-d's intent in creation, the
establishment of a dwelling in this material world, is not
merely an objective to which we should strive, but one
which should be internalized within our own selves. And
as this motive blossoms into fulfillment, every person can
perceive its benefits; his existence is thus "better for him."

PERCEIVING TRUTH WHICH TRANSCENDS INTELLECT As mentioned at the outset, although the Torah leaves room for a variety of theoretical approaches, with regard to actual practice, our *halachic* tradition has always striven toward uniformity. In this vein, our Sages teach:[49]

> From three years, there was a difference of opinion between the School of Shammai and the School of Hillel. These would say, "The *halachah* follows our perspective," and these would say, "The *halachah* follows our perspective."
>
> A heavenly voice issued forth: "These and these are the words of the living G-d; the *halachah* follows the School of *Hillel.*"

The passage continues:

> Why did the School of Hillel merit to have the *halachah* follow their perspective? Because they were patient and humble, and would cite the statements of the School of Shammai before their own.

The latter passage is difficult to understand. Our Sages state that the students of the School of Shammai were more astute and discriminating[50] than the students of the School of Hillel. Since the comprehension of Torah law depends on intellectual understanding, seemingly it would be appropriate for the *halachah* to follow their perspective. Moreover, the rationale given by the *Talmud,* that the students of the School of Hillel were "patient and humble" is problematic. What connection do these virtues have with the determination of law?

---

49. *Eruvin, loc. cit.*
50. *Yevamos* 14a; *Tosafos, Eruvin* 6b.

These difficulties can, however, be resolved by differentiating between Torah study and other fields of wisdom. The Torah is not merely knowledge; the Torah is unbounded G-dly truth. Its intellectual dimension is merely a garb that enables man to internalize his connection with this truth.

Wisdom can be grasped through intellect. To develop a connection with the Torah's unbounded truth, however, intellect is not sufficient: *bittul,* self-transcending commitment, is necessary. The patience and humility of the School of Hillel reflects such *bittul.* And for this reason, it is their perspective which determines the *halachah.*

DETERMINING **HALACHAH** To offer an explanation of the above passage which relates more closely to the principles of Torah law:[51] The *halachah* follows the School of Hillel, because except for several isolated instances, a majority of Sages followed their understanding. Nevertheless, since the School of Shammai were more astute, the Sages doubted whether they should rely on the majority vote. And it was not until the proclamation of the heavenly voice that these doubts were silenced.[52]

One might ask: If the Sages of the School of Shammai were more astute, why didn't the majority of Sages accept their rulings? Because a ruling of Torah law must be understood thoroughly by the Sage delivering it. Although the Sages of the School of Shammai were more astute, the majority of the Sages could not thoroughly comprehend

51. See *Tosafos, loc. cit.*
52. Although *halachah* cannot be determined on the basis of a heavenly voice *(Bava Metzia* 59b), this principle applies when the heavenly voice contradicts the ruling of the majority, and not when it supports it *(Tosafos).*

their logic, and therefore they could not rule accordingly. To cite a parallel example — extending the wording slightly beyond its literal context, our Sages state:[53]

> There was no one in Rabbi Meir's generation of his stature. Why then was the *halachah* not established according to his perspective? Because his colleagues could not comprehend the full breadth of his knowledge.

Because the logic advanced by Rabbi Meir and the School of Shammai could not be grasped fully by their colleagues, the rulings they rendered were not accepted as law.

Also, from a spiritual perspective, the approach of the School of Hillel — spreading light — is vital in the present age to elevate mankind and the world at large. It is true that this endeavor presents challenges. The words of caution of the School of Shammai must be, therefore, included within our spiritual consciousness, but our overriding attitude should be one of positive activity.

LOOKING TOWARD THE HORIZON Although in the present age, the *halachah* follows the School of Hillel, in the Era of the Redemption, the *halachah* will follow the School of Shammai.[54] In that era, "the Jews will be great sages, and know the hidden matters."[55] The majority of the Sages will thus comprehend the perspective of the School of Shammai, and therefore, the *halachah* will change.[56] Moreover,

---

53. *Eruvin* 13b.
54. *Mikdash Melech* to *Zohar*, Vol. I, 17b; *Likkutei Torah, Korach,* p. 54b ff.
55. *Rambam, Mishneh Torah, Hilchos Melachim* 12:5.
56. For although as stated above (note 11), a later court cannot change a ruling adopted by a previous court unless "it is greater than its prede-

since *Mashiach* will "perfect the entire world,"[57] the task of refinement given the Jewish people will be different in that era, and the more elevated standard required by the School of Shammai will be accessible to people at large.

At the present time, short moments before the dawning of that future era, we should yearn to be able to apply the lofty standards of refinement taught by the School of Shammai. Simultaneously, however, we must realize that the means to hasten the coming of that era is the warm and humble outreach exemplified by the School of Hillel.

<hr>

cessors in wisdom and in the number of adherents it has," the *Sanhedrin* to be convened by *Mashiach* will surely meet those qualifications.

57. *Rambam, Mishneh Torah, loc. cit.* 11:4.

Immanence and Transcendence:

An Analysis of the Differences in Approach Between Rabbi Yishmael and Rabbi Akiva

Adapted from *Hadranim al HaShas*, Vol. I, p. 55ff.;
Likkutei Sichos, Vol. VI, p. 119ff.

BLESSINGS FOR SACRIFICIAL OFFERINGS

The concluding *mishnah* of the tractate of *Pesachim* states:

"If one recites the blessing over the Paschal sacrifice, one satisfies the requirement for the [Chagigah] offering. If one recites the blessing over the [Chagigah] offering, one does not satisfy the requirement for the Paschal sacrifice," these are the words of Rabbi Yishmael.

Rabbi Akiva says: "[The blessing for] one does not satisfy the requirement for the other, nor does [the blessing for] the other satisfy the requirement for the first."

Rabbi Chayim Cohen[1] (based on the *Jerusalem Talmud*[2]) explains that Rabbi Yishmael's opinion is based on his conception of the Paschal sacrifice as being of fundamental importance *(ikkar)* and the *Chagigah* offering as being of secondary importance *(tafel)*. Thus, by reciting the blessing over the *ikkar,* one satisfies the requirement of the blessing for the *tafel.*[3]

This explanation raises an obvious question with regard to Rabbi Akiva's position. For seemingly, everyone would agree that the *Chagigah* offering is of secondary importance to the Paschal sacrifice. (For there is no inherent obligation to bring a *Chagigah* sacrifice on the 14th of Nissan. Why is it brought? Only because one must eat the Paschal sacrifice when one's appetite has been satiated. To satisfy that requirement, the *Chagigah* offering is usually[4] eaten first.[5])

Why then does Rabbi Akiva not accept Rabbi Yishmael's view? It is a universally accepted principle that if one recites a blessing over a matter of fundamental importance, one satisfies the requirement for reciting a blessing over a matter of secondary importance.[6]

---

1.   Cited by *Tosafos, Pesachim* 121a.
2.   The conclusion of *Pesachim.*
3.   With this interpretation, Rabbi Chayim Cohen shifts the emphasis from the debate in the *Babylonian Talmud* which focuses on whether pouring *(shefichah)* the blood on the altar is considered as throwing it *(zerikah),* or conversely whether throwing the blood is considered as pouring it.

   The *Tzelach* uses Rabbi Chayim Cohen's interpretation to resolve an apparent contradiction between the *Rambam's* ruling in *Hilchos Chametz UMatzah* 8:7 and his ruling in *Hilchos Pesulei HaMukdashim* 2:3. See the gloss of the *Lechem Mishneh* to *Hilchos Chametz UMatzah.*
4.   This applies when the *Chagigah* offering is sacrificed. There are, however, instances when we do not bring a *Chagigah* offering. See the sources listed in the following note.
5.   *Pesachim* 69b; *Rambam, Mishneh Torah, Hilchos Korban Pesach* 10:12.
6.   *Berachos* 44a; *Rambam, Mishneh Torah, Hilchos Berachos* 3:5.

EVERY
***MITZVAH* HAS**
INTEGRAL
IMPORTANCE

Rabbi Akiva's position can be explained as follows: With regard to eating for personal satisfaction, there is a difference between matters of primary importance and matters of secondary importance. For it is the person's own will which determines the relative importance of an object. With regard to *mitzvos,* by contrast, there is no concept of primary and secondary importance, as we are commanded:[7] "Do not sit and weigh [the importance of] the *mitzvos* of the Torah."

Thus it is true that the *Chagigah* offering is required only for the sake of the Paschal sacrifice, and there are times when it is not offered. Nevertheless, whenever it is offered, since it is required and it is a *mitzvah* to partake of it, it not a secondary matter and requires a blessing of its own.

Indeed, Rabbi Yishmael also accepts the fundamental premise of this approach. For even according to Rabbi Yishmael, at the outset, a separate blessing should be

---

It is possible to explain Rabbi Akiva's position as follows: Since the *Chagigah* offering is eaten before the Paschal sacrifice, a blessing must be recited upon it, for as the *Ramah (Orach Chayim* 212:1) states when one eats an object which is *tafel* before the object which is *ikkar,* a blessing is required. This, however, raises a question with regard to Rabbi Yishmael's position: Since the *Chagigah* offering is eaten first, how can it be covered by the blessing recited afterwards on the Paschal sacrifice?

To this, it can be explained that the *Ramah's* principle mentioned above applies with regard to eating for personal satisfaction. Different principles apply with regard to the subject at hand: the blessings recited before performing a *mitzvah.* In this instance, since the *Chagigah* offering is secondary to the Paschal sacrifice, seemingly there is no need for a separate blessing. This justification of Rabbi Yishmael's position, however, raises again the original question with regard to Rabbi Akiva's position.

7.   *Devarim Rabbah* 6:2.

recited for the *Chagigah* offering.[8] It is only after the fact
that he rules that the blessing for the Paschal sacrifice also
satisfies the requirement for the *Chagigah* offering.

**WHERE THE
MITZVOS
ORIGINATED**
According to this explanation, the difference between Rabbi Akiva and Rabbi Yishmael does not concern merely a particular point, but rather reflects a general difference in approach which finds expression in many contexts. For Rabbi Akiva's position is that every *mitzvah* is of inherent and indigenous importance, while Rabbi Yishmael maintains that there is a certain degree of primacy between *mitzvos;* some have greater importance than others.

Thus we find that with regard to the manner in which the *mitzvos* were communicated to the Jewish people, we also find a difference of opinion between Rabbi Yishmael and Rabbi Akiva.[9] Rabbi Yishmael maintains that the general categories of *mitzvos* were given at Mount Sinai. The particular *mitzvos,* by contrast, were given to Moshe in the Tent of Meeting. Rabbi Akiva differs and maintains that both the general categories and the particular *mitzvos* were given at Mount Sinai. Afterwards, the particular *mitzvos* were repeated to Moshe in the Tent of Meeting.

Since Rabbi Yishmael differentiates between the importance of the particular *mitzvos,* he has no difficulty seeing some — those which are of general importance — as having been given at Sinai, while others — those of a more particular nature — to have been given afterwards.

---

8. While with regard to the recitation of a blessing over a secondary food, it is forbidden to recite a blessing over the secondary food if one has recited a blessing over the primary food.
9. *Sotah* 37b.

Rabbi Akiva, by contrast, because he emphasizes the inherent importance of each and every *mitzvah,* appreciates every *mitzvah* as originating in the essential revelation of G-dliness at Sinai. In this, there is no distinction between one *mitzvah* and another.

WHAT THE PEOPLE SAID AT SINAI   Another difference of opinion involving these two Sages concerns the very revelation at Sinai itself. The Torah introduces the Ten Commandments with the verse,[10] "And G-d spoke all these words, saying...." Our Sages[11] explain the word *leimor* ("saying") as indicating that the Jews responded to G-d after each commandment.[12] As to the actual response, there is a difference of opinion among our Sages: Rabbi Yishmael states that they answered "Yes" to the positive commandments and "No" to the negative ones; Rabbi Akiva maintains that they answered "Yes" to all the commandments, signifying their willingness to fulfill G-d's will in every detail.

Rabbi Yishmael focuses on the practical application of the *mitzvos.* Thus he maintains that the Jews responded in a manner which reflects the manner in which the *mitzvos* are observed and answered: "Yes" to the positive commandments and "No" to the negative commandments. Rabbi Akiva, by contrast, focuses on the greater purpose

---

10. *Shmos* 20:1.

11. *Mechilta* on this verse.

12. Generally, the word *leimor* is understood as meaning "to convey"; i.e., G-d gave Moshe a commandment to convey to the Jewish people as a whole (see *Rashi* on *Shmos* 19:2 and elsewhere). However, this meaning is not appropriate for the present verse, because all the Jews were present at Mount Sinai. Indeed, our Sages *(Shmos Rabbah* 28:6) teach that even the souls of the Jews of all future generations were present at the Giving of the Torah.

common to all *mitzvos* and not on the particular details of the individual *mitzvos*. For this reason, he sees the Jewish people's answer as expressing an undifferentiated commitment. By saying "Yes" to both the positive and negative commandments, they demonstrated an unbounded commitment to fulfill G-d's will.[13]

In the three examples given above, Rabbi Yishmael's perspective focuses on the Torah as it provides the functional guidelines for the Divine service of the Jewish people. Therefore, his perspective recognizes differences between *mitzvos* of primary importance and those of secondary importance, between general categories and particular *mitzvos,* and between positive and negative commandments.

Rabbi Akiva's perspective, by contrast, focuses on the Torah as it reflects G-d's will. And from this perspective, there is no distinction between the *mitzvos,* for they all equally express His essential oneness.

WHAT THEY SAW AT SINAI Another difference of opinion between these two Sages regarding the revelation at Sinai clarifies further their differences in approach. Rabbi Yishmael[14] interprets the verse:[15] "All the people saw the sounds and the flames," as meaning that the people "saw what is usually seen, and heard what is usually heard." In his reading, the verb "saw" does not apply to the object "sounds" which

---

13. Saying "Yes" to the negative commandments also hints at the possibility of transforming the negative dimensions of our experience, as practiced in the Divine service of Rabbi Akiva as will be explained in note 29.

14. *Mechilta* on the verse below.

15. *Shmos* 20:15.

follows it immediately, but only to "flames" which is the second object of the verb in the verse.

Rabbi Akiva, however, maintains that the verb's direct object is also its semantic object. In his reading, the Giving of the Torah brought about an upheaval within the natural order; the people "heard what is usually seen and saw what is usually heard." They saw the sounds and heard the flames.

What is the difference between seeing and hearing? Witnessing an event makes such a powerful impression on a person that he cannot be persuaded that it has not taken place.[16] Sound, by contrast, does not make as powerful an impression: a person who hears an idea is still capable of imagining a conflicting position.

On this basis, we can appreciate the Sages' understanding of the events of Sinai. Rabbi Akiva views the purpose of the Torah as transforming a person's frame of reference, drawing him away from involvement in worldly matters and connecting him to G-d's will. In his reading of the verse, this is what the Jews actually experienced at Sinai. Their senses were reoriented and they "saw" the spiritual and "heard" the material.

What made a deep and lasting impression upon them was the spiritual, that which is usually "heard." And at that time, they related only abstractly to material things, merely "hearing" that which is ordinarily "seen."

Rabbi Yishmael conceives of the Torah's purpose differently, seeing it as having a downward thrust that enables G-dliness to permeate nature. In his view, the Torah is not intended to make man rise above the

---

16. For this reason our Sages maintain that a person who has seen an event cannot objectively consider a defendant's rights; hence the rule (Rosh HaShanah 26a) that "a witness cannot serve as a judge."

framework of worldly experience, but instead, to make that framework, intact within its natural pattern, reflect G-dliness. Therefore, he maintains, the Jews "saw what is usually seen and heard what is usually heard." This was not, however, an ordinary form of seeing and hearing. At Sinai, the Jews were able to see and hear G-dliness as it pervades the natural order.

HOW THE TORAH CHOOSES TO SPEAK
A similar pattern is also reflected in these two Sages' approach to Biblical exegesis. Frequently, the Torah will repeat a verb, for example:[17] הכרת תכרת. כרת means "to cut off." Rabbi Yishmael[18] maintains that "the Torah speaks in the language of men." As such, just as mortal writers will use repetition for emphasis, so too, the Torah. According to his conception, the above phrase means: "He will certainly be cut off."

Rabbi Akiva, by contrast, considers each word used by the Torah as a significant Divine message. In his conception, repetition is not a mere literary technique, but an invitation for exegesis. Thus he interprets this phrase as meaning: "הכרת —He will be cut off in this world (i.e., die prematurely); תכרת — He will be cut off in the World to Come (and not merit the spiritual rewards of that era)."[19]

A similar pattern is reflected in their interpretation of the prohibition:[20] "Do not curse אלהים." Rabbi Yishmael maintains that אלהים refers to a judge in our mortal

---

17. *Bamidbar* 15:31.
18. *Sanhedrin* 90b.
19. See *Tosafos, Sotah* 24b which gives several other examples of differences in interpretation between Rabbi Akiva and Rabbi Yishmael revolving around this principle.
20. *Shmos* 22:27.

sphere. Rabbi Akiva, by contrast, interprets א-להים as referring to the ultimate Judge, G-d.

In both these instances, Rabbi Yishmael's approach to interpretation sees the Torah as reaching down into the mortal frame of reference, "speaking in the language of man," so that our worldly experience could be permeated by G-dliness. Rabbi Akiva, by contrast, conceives of the Torah as spiritual truth, above the mortal realm of experience, and appreciates it as a medium to enable man to elevate himself, and attain this higher standard.

REQUIRED OR LEFT TO MAN'S CHOICE
This same motif is reflected in these Sages' interpretations of several Biblical commandments. For example, with regard to a priest becoming ritually impure for the burial of his close relatives, the Torah states:[21] "For her, he shall become impure." With regard to the treatment of Canaanite servants, it is written:[22] "You will work with them forever." And with regard to a person issuing a warning to his wife with regard to her moral conduct, it is written:[23] "He shall adjure his wife."

In all these instances, Rabbi Yishmael maintains[24] that the matter is left to the choice of the person involved. If he desires, he may become impure, maintain ownership of his servants, or adjure his wife. Or he may choose not to. The Torah is merely providing him with options; it his decision whether to employ them or not. Rabbi Akiva, by contrast, maintains that these are all mandatory com-

21. *Vayikra* 21:3.
22. *Ibid.,* 25:48.
23. *Bamidbar* 5:14.
24. *Sotah* 3a.

mands, obligations that must be fulfilled without leaving any room for a person's choice.

In these instances as well, since Rabbi Yishmael conceives of the Torah as reaching down into the mortal frame of reference, he maintains that it recognizes the importance of man's choice and grants him options. In this way, the Torah becomes internalized within a person's mind and thought.

Rabbi Akiva, by contrast, sees the Torah as a G-dly standard that gives man an opportunity to rise above his mortality. Accordingly, he sees its goal, not in granting man options in how to exercise his will, but rather in giving him the chance to transcend his own will entirely, and accept G-d's.

THE SOURCE FOR THE PATTERN   These two perspectives flow from basic differences in the approaches of the two Sages. Rabbi Yishmael was a *Kohen;* according to some views, even a High Priest.[25] Because his world was one of holiness, he perceived his challenge in the service of G-d to be the extension of the borders of holiness, drawing G-dliness into the framework of worldly existence.[26]

---

25. See *Rashi* on *Chullin* 49a cited by *Seder HaDoros, Maareches* R. Yishmael, ch. 8.

26. On this basis, we can understand Rabbi Yishmael's position in a renown *Talmudic* passage *(Berachos 35b):*

"It is written *(Devarim 11:14):* 'And you shall gather your grain.' What is the intent? It is also written *(Yehoshua 1:8):* 'This Torah scroll should not depart from your mouths.' Should the latter verse be applied literally? [For this reason,] it is written: 'And you shall gather your grain,' teaching that one must follow the way of the world," these are the words of Rabbi Yishmael.

Rabbi Akiva, by contrast, stemmed from a family of converts[27] and did not himself begin studying Torah until he was forty.[28] His approach to Divine service reflected the striving of the *baal teshuvah,* who rises above himself and his previous experiences and turns to G-d.[29]

Rabbi Shimon bar Yochai [Rabbi Akiva's student] states: "Is it possible that a man will [devote his time and energy] to plowing and sowing?... What will become of the Torah?"

The *Talmud* continues: "Many followed Rabbi Yishmael's approach and were successful. Many followed Rabbi Shimon's approach and were not successful." But Rabbi Yishmael's intent is not merely to teach a more practical approach. Instead, his goal is that our mode of Divine service should emphasize bringing Torah observance into the context of worldly reality, not transcending that reality by clinging to the spiritual.

27. *Seder HaDoros;* the *Rambam's* Introduction to the *Mishneh Torah.*
28. *Avos deRabbi Nosan* 6:2.
29. Rabbi Akiva's drive to transcend his immediate circumstances and appreciate the inner G-dly message of every particular event may be seen in the following narrative (the conclusion of Tractate *Makkos*).

    Some time after the Second Destruction, he and four other Sages were making their way up to Jerusalem. As they cleared the summit of Mt. Scopus, the desolate sight of the Holy City met their eyes, and they rent their garments. Approaching the Temple Mount they saw a fox prowling through the ruins of the Holy of Holies. Four scholars wept; Rabbi Akiva alone radiated joy.

    The Sages asked him, "Why are you joyful?" Whereupon he asked them, "And why do you weep?"

    They answered: "In the very Sanctuary which was permitted to the High Priest alone, foxes now roam — then shall we not weep?"

    Replied Rabbi Akiva: "And for that very reason I laugh.... In the Book of *Michah* (3:12) it is written, 'Therefore shall Zion for your sake be plowed like a field.' In the Book of *Zechariah* (8:4), it is written, 'Old men and old women shall yet sit in the streets of Jerusalem.' Until the first prophecy was fulfilled, I may have doubted the truth of the second. Now that the first prophecy has indeed been fulfilled, we may rely with absolute certainty that the second will also come true!"

    Rabbi Akiva was able to look beyond the immediate situation and perceive the inner G-dly truth at its core. This is characteristic of the manner in which he sought to rise above the limits of his worldly experience.

THE ERA OF THE REDEMPTION: A SYNTHESIS OF BOTH APPROACHES The ultimate goal of our Divine service is a combination of these two approaches, for each has its distinctive merits. This synthesis will reach its apex in the Era of the Redemption, when "*Mashiach* will motivate the righteous to turn to G-d in *teshuvah*."[30] The Divine service of "the righteous," which is directed towards drawing down G-dliness within the context of the natural order (Rabbi Yishmael's mode of Divine service), will be permeated by the all-encompassing commitment evoked by *teshuvah* (Rabbi Akiva's path).

Since we are living in the time immediately before the coming of *Mashiach,* we can appreciate a foretaste of this synthesis in our time. Through these efforts, we will hasten the coming of the time when we will achieve the ultimate expression of both these approaches, with the coming of *Mashiach.* May this take place in the immediate future.

---

30. *Likkutei Torah, Shemini Atzeres,* p. 92b; *Zohar,* Vol. III, p. 153b.

WHAT MAKES THE SCALES OF JUDGMENT TIP?

AN ANALYSIS OF THE CONTRAST BETWEEN THE POSITIONS OF RABBAN GAMLIEL AND THE SAGES

Adapted from *Likkutei Sichos,* Vol. XXIV, p. 95ff.

THE DEFINITION OF COMMUNAL PRAYER The tractate of *Rosh HaShanah* concludes with the following *mishnah:*[1]

Just as the *chazzan*[2] is obligated to recite [the *Shemoneh Esreh*], each and every individual is obligated [to recite the *Shemoneh Esreh*].

Rabban Gamliel states: "The *chazzan* fulfills the obligation on behalf of the community."

---

1. *Rosh HaShanah* 33b.
2. The exact term used is *shliach tzibbur,* "the representative of the community."

In the explanation of that *mishnah*, the *Gemara* cites a *beraisa*:[3]

> [The Sages] told Rabban Gamliel: "According to your conception, why does the community recite [the *Shemoneh Esreh*] prayers [individually]?
>
> He answered them: "To allow the *chazzan* to prepare his prayers."
>
> Rabban Gamliel asked [the Sages]: "According to your conception, why does the *chazzan* recite a communal prayer?"
>
> They answered him: "To fulfill the obligation on behalf of a person who does not know [how to recite the prayers himself]."
>
> He replied: "Just as he fulfills the obligation on behalf of a person who does not know [how to recite the prayers himself], he fulfills the obligation on behalf of a person who knows [how to recite the prayers himself]."

According to the conception of Rabbeinu Asher, the difference of opinion between Rabban Gamliel and the Sages focuses on the definition of communal prayer. Our Sages define communal prayer as the community praying together, i.e., rather than praying individually, every member of the community prays together with his colleagues. The *chazzan's* repetition of the prayers is an incidental measure: Since there are some individuals who do not know how to pray themselves, the *chazzan* recites the prayers on their behalf.

Rabban Gamliel, by contrast, maintains that the fundamental element of communal prayer is the prayer

---

3. *Ibid.*, 34b.

recited by the *chazzan* on behalf of the entire congregation. The only reason every person prays individually before the *chazzan's* recitation of the *Shemoneh Esreh* is to enable the *chazzan* to prepare himself to pray.[4]

| **QUALITY OR** | This difference of opinion between the |
| **QUANTITY** | Sages and Rabban Gamliel is not |

merely an isolated issue, but instead reflects a difference of a more encompassing scope between their conceptual approaches. From the following incident related by the *Talmud*,[5] we can appreciate the issues motivating their difference of opinion.

While Rabban Gamliel was *Nasi*, he would proclaim: "Any student whose inner core does not reflect his external appearance should not enter the House of Study," and he appointed a watchman at the door to ensure that this approach was followed.

After Rabban Gamliel was replaced by Rabbi Elazar ben Azariah, the watchman was removed, and unrestricted license was granted for students to attend. On that day, hundreds of new students entered, and the House of Study became engrossed in a sequence of unusually productive intellectual interchanges.

What is the core of the difference between the two positions? Rabban Gamliel focused on maintaining the

---

4. The *Rambam* obviously has another conception of the difference of opinion between the Sages and Rabban Gamliel. For in the *Mishneh Torah, Hilchos Tefillah* 8:4, he defines communal prayer as follows: "What is communal prayer? That one person recite the prayers out loud and the others listen." Nevertheless *(ibid.:9)*, he follows the Sages' conception that the *chazzan* fulfills the obligation of prayer only on behalf of those who are unable to recite the prayers themselves. See also the comments of Rabbeinu Nissim to *Rosh HaShanah, loc. cit.*

5. *Berachos* 28a.

quality of the students of the House of Study. If a student did not possess the moral caliber appropriate for a Torah scholar, Rabban Gamliel barred him from attending the House of Study. Although the quantity of the students would be reduced, the standards of quality would be maintained.

The Sages, whose perspective was put into expression by Rabbi Elazar ben Azariah, on the other hand, put the emphasis on the quantity of students. Although there would be students of lower caliber — and at the outset, this might detract from the level of the House of Study as a whole[6] — it was worth making this sacrifice to expose more students to the Torah.

OUT OF THE MANY, ONE   To illustrate these positions with regard to the previous discussion concerning prayer: Communal prayer possesses two advantages over individual prayer: a) one of quantity; there are more individuals praying at the same time, and b) one of quality; these individuals are forged together into a new entity of which it can be said: The whole exceeds the sum of its parts. The communal entity which emerges is not merely a composite of individuals,

---

6.   From a different perspective, it can be argued that the emphasis on quantity will not necessarily detract from quality. On the contrary, it is possible that the numerous different approaches will produce a synergistic dynamism that will increase growth. This is reflected in the passage from the *Talmud* cited above which states that: "That day, there was not an issue in the House of Study that was left unresolved, without interpretation." As *Rashi* comments: "Since the number of students increased, the discussion and honing of perception was also amplified."

but rather a new integrate which exists within a totally different frame of reference.[7]

Our Sages, who emphasize quantity, focus on the congregation, whose members join together their individual prayers. Rabban Gamliel, by contrast, underscores the advantage of the prayer of the *chazzan*, the *shliach tzibbur*. For his prayer is of a different nature entirely. The accent is not on his individual level of refinement — although a *chazzan* should possess such qualities as well[8] — but on the fact that his prayer is the prayer of the community at large. It is as if every word that he recites is being recited by this communal entity as one.[9]

IS AN OATH REQUIRED? The contrast between the priorities chosen by Rabban Gamliel and the Sages also relates to a ruling within a totally different context. The *mishnah* states:[10]

> [When a plaintiff] claims that [the defendant] owes him wheat, and [the defendant] admits owing him barley, [the defendant] is not liable [to take an oath]. Rabban Gamliel maintains that he is liable.

The oath in question is the oath required when a defendant is *modeh bemiktzas*, i.e., he admits liability to a portion of the claim which is made of him. To incur this oath, the defendant's admission must relate to the claim made of him. If he admits a liability of a different type, he

---

7. See the *K'lallei HaTorah VehaMitzvos* from the Rogatchover Gaon, *erech tzibbur*, which discusses several unique dimensions of a communal entity.

8. See *Taanis* 16a; *Tur* and *Shulchan Aruch (Orach Chayim*, ch. 53).

9. See the *Shulchan Aruch HaRav* 213:6, where when speaking about one person reciting a blessing on behalf of another, the Alter Rebbe uses the expression "He is their agent,... and his mouth is as their mouths."

10. *Shavuos* 38b.

is not required to take this oath. Thus, according to the Sages, when the defendant admits to owing the plaintiff barley, he is not considered to be admitting part of the claim, for his admission concerns a different matter altogether. To quote our Sages:[11] "What he claimed, the other did not admit, and what he admitted, the other did not claim." The defendant denies entirely the claim that he owes the plaintiff wheat — and when a person denies a claim entirely, he is not required to take an oath according to Scriptural law. The fact that he adds that he owes the plaintiff barley is of no consequence whatsoever.

Why do the Sages reach this conclusion? Quantity, their emphasis in the instances mentioned above, relates to the material dimension of the objects or persons involved.[12] And when one looks from a material perspective, wheat and barley are two different entities.

In the instances mentioned above, by contrast, Rabban Gamliel highlights the quality, which relates to the abstract nature of the object or persons. And when one looks abstractly, whether one is claiming that it is wheat or barley which is owed, the fundamental point is the same: A debt, an obligation that has a direct, financial counterpart, exists. Therefore, Rabban Gamliel maintains that, although there is a difference between the subject of the debt which is claimed and the admission that is made, the defendant is still admitting to owing a portion of what the plaintiff claims. Therefore, an oath is required.

---

11. *Ibid.*
12. To explain the above using the terminology employed in *yeshivos:* *Kamos* (quantity) relates to *chomer* (an object's material dimension), while *eichos* (quality) relates to *tzurah* (an entity's abstract form, its content and import).

WHAT	Another difference of opinion be-
MOTIVATES	tween Rabban Gamliel and the
GENEROSITY?	Sages is reflected in the interpreta-

tions which they offer for the verse:[13] "The kindness
[offered by the gentile] nations is deficient."[14] There are
several interpretations offered by the *Talmud.*[15] Rabbi
Eliezer states that the gentiles offer generosity in order to
receive "greatness" (interpreted by the *Maharsha,*[16] to refer
to long life). Rabbi Yehoshua states that they offer kindness, "so that their dominion will continue [to prevail]."
And Rabban Gamliel states that the reason for their kindness is "to take pride."

Rabbi Eliezer and Rabbi Yehoshua explain that the
deficiency in the gentiles' approach to kindness and
charity is that they give in order to receive. They realize
that their good deeds will lead to reward, and that is their
intent. Rabban Gamliel, by contrast, explains that their
fault relates more to individual ethics; they are seeking
personal aggrandizement, and give only for that reason.

The differences between these two approaches is an
outgrowth of the concepts mentioned above. To explain:
Every act of kindness or charity serves two purposes: a) to
meet the need felt by the recipient; b) to lift his spirits
through the expression of feelings of empathy and com-
passion. And the second dimension is greater, as our
Sages teach:[17] "A person who gives a coin to a poor person

---

13. *Mishlei* 14:34.
14. Our translation follows the commentary of the *Ralbag,* and is evident
    from the interpretation of the word חסאים in *I Melachim* 1:21. There
    are, however, other interpretations of the term חסאת used by the *Tal-*
    mud.
15. *Bava Basra* 10b.
16. *Chiddushei Aggados.*
17. *Bava Basra* 9b.

is granted six blessings; one who gratifies him is blessed elevenfold." Meeting the person's needs involves a material gift, while gratifying him involves giving him something intangible.

On this basis, we can see the connection to the concepts mentioned above: Rabbi Eliezer and Rabbi Yehoshua, the leaders of the Sages who differ with Rabban Gamliel, put the emphasis on the material benefit provided by acts of kindness (the quantity one receives). Since the gentiles are concerned with the reward their generosity will bring them and not the needs of the recipient, there will be a deficiency in their gifts, and they will not satisfy the recipients' needs completely.

Rabban Gamliel, by contrast, puts the emphasis on the quality of the gifts, the feelings which the giver conveys. Since the gentiles are motivated by their own self-aggrandizement, they cannot properly empathize with the recipient, and there will always be deficiency in the relationship established.

MAKING DISTINCTIONS One of the principles of *Talmudic* study is the avoidance of redundancy. A concept is stated once. If it is repeated, there must be a reason for the repetition, a difference between the two cases which necessitates the restatement of the principle in the second context. This is reflected in the *Talmudic* construct, *utzericha,* in which a distinction is made between two instances in which a principle is stated.

Similarly, with regard to the concepts above: We must be able to explain why each of the illustrations of the differences in perspective between Rabban Gamliel and the Sages are necessary.

The first two instances concern the realms of Torah study and prayer. With regard to the quality of Torah scholars, our Sages state:[18] "A Torah scholar whose inner core does not reflect his external appearance is not a Torah scholar at all." With regard to prayer, by contrast, although the prayers of a *chazzan* reflect a higher level than the individual prayers of the community, the individual prayers of the community are still significant, for they possess two advantages: a) quantity, and b) quality. (Although these prayers are not on the level of the *chazzan's* prayer, they still exceed the quality of the prayers that an individual recites alone.)

Therefore, were Rabban Gamliel's emphasis on quality to be expressed only with regard to the caliber of Torah students, we would be unable to draw any conclusions with regard to prayer. For a student who lacks the level of refinement required by Rabban Gamliel is not considered significant at all. With regard to the individual prayers of the community, by contrast, we might think that the combination of quantity and quality expressed by the individual prayers of the community would override the higher quality possessed by the prayers of the *chazzan*. Hence, the need for the statement of both points.

Conversely, were Rabban Gamliel's opinion to be stated only with regard to communal prayer: a) we would need to mention the case of the qualifications for Torah study to express the position of the Sages,[19] and b) we

18. *Yoma* 72b.
19. I.e., that even a student who initially lacks moral virtue should be allowed to enter the House of Study. Indeed, the perspective of the Sages can be taken as a directive, one which is particularly applicable in the present age. Even if initially, a student lacks virtue, he should be encouraged to attend the House of Study, for through that attendance, he will acquire that virtue.

would not know Rabban Gamliel's opinion with regard to Torah study. For success in Torah study comes through "close association with colleagues, and sharp discussion with students."[20] One might think that some sacrifice might be made with regard to the caliber of the students so that the increased number of students would add to the intensity and vibrancy of the discussion. Hence, it was necessary to mention Rabban Gamliel's opinion in this area as well.

| **THE SPIRITUAL** | Continuing the development of |
| **AND THE MATERIAL** | these concepts, it is also neces- |

sary to explain why once the positions of Rabban Gamliel and the Sages are expressed with regard to Torah study and prayer, it is required to restate them with regard to oaths and charity. It is possible to explain that since Torah study and prayer are primarily spiritual activities, it is apparent why Rabban Gamliel places an emphasis on quality with regard to them. With regard to claims regarding material objects, by contrast, one might think that he would agree that the emphasis could be placed on the material dimensions of the articles. Hence, it is necessary to restate Rabban Gamliel's position in this context as well.

Conversely, if the difference of opinion was only stated with regard to oaths, we would not be able to appreciate the Sages' opinion with regard to Torah study and prayer. For it might be presumed that in that context, they would accept Rabban Gamliel's emphasis on quality.

---

20. *Avos* 6:1.

THE DIFFERENCE BETWEEN DEEDS OF KINDNESS AND TORAH STUDY AND PRAYER

Similarly, it can be explained that with regard to kindness and charity, what is of fundamental importance is that the needy person receive the assistance which he is lacking. For this reason, our Sages state:[21] "When a person loses a coin..., and it is found by a poor person who uses it for his livelihood, it is considered as if he acted meritoriously." In this instance, the "donor" had no intent of assisting the recipient at all; his gift was made totally involuntarily. Nevertheless, since the recipient derived benefit, the donor attains merit.

With regard to prayer and Torah study, the "quality," the spiritual content of the act is inseparable from the act itself. For when a person studies (the Oral Law),[22] he does not derive any merit from his study unless he understands its content. So too with regard to prayer, proper intention — the awareness that one is praying to G-d — is of fundamental importance. Without such intention, one's prayer is not acceptable.[23]

For this reason, were Rabban Gamliel's opinion to be stated only with regard to prayer and study, one might think that with regard to charity and deeds of kindness, where quantity is more important, he would accept the position of the other Sages. Conversely, were his opinion to be stated only with regard to charity and deeds of kindness, his position with regard to prayer and Torah study could not be known.

---

21. *Sifri, Ki Seitzei* 24:19.
22. *Shulchan Aruch HaRav, Hilchos Talmud Torah,* the conclusion of ch. 2.
23. See *Rambam, Mishneh Torah, Hilchos Tefillah* 4:15-16. Note the discussion of these concepts in *Likkutei Sichos,* Vol. XXII, p. 117ff.

For with regard to charity, the emphasis on quality does not detract from the quantity, while with regard to Torah study and prayer, by highlighting the quality, one actually reduces the quantity. For by restricting the entry of students to those "whose inner core reflects their external appearance," Rabban Gamliel lowered the number of students attending the House of Study. And by putting the emphasis on the prayers of the *chazzan,* the prayers of the many are replaced by one communal prayer.[24] It is thus necessary to state Rabban Gamliel's opinion in these instances to show that even when the emphasis on quality is to the exclusion of quantity, his position remains unchanged.

THE SOURCE OF MOTIVATION

This more encompassing conception of the difference between the approaches of Rabban Gamliel and the Sages has its source in the positions they held. Rabban Gamliel was the *Nasi,* the leader of the *Sanhedrin.* The *Nasi* was not a democratic leader. Instead, as implied by that name which means "uplifted one," his position resembled that of a king. The authority of a *Nasi* or a king does not stem from a quantitative advantage, but is a result of the elevated spiritual quality which the king or the *Nasi* represents.

This concept is emphasized by *Rashi,*[25] who states: "The *Nasi* is the entire people." To refer to the example of

---

24. Similarly, by appreciating the converse of these arguments, it can be appreciated why the positions of the Sages with regard to Torah study and prayer would not enable us to determine their views with regard to deeds of kindness, and why their positions with regard to deeds of kindness are not an adequate indicator with regard to their views regarding Torah study and prayer.

25. In his commentary to *Bamidbar* 21:21.

the *chazzan* mentioned above, his prayers were not those of his individual self, but rather those of the community at large. Similarly, the *Nasi* does not act as an individual, but as the representative of the Jewish people as a collective. For this reason, Rabban Gamliel, who served as *Nasi,* placed an emphasis on quality.

The Sages, by contrast, were members of the *Sanhedrin.* Their power stemmed from quantity, as reflected in the fact that in order for the *Sanhedrin* to hold session, a quorum of 36 judges, the majority of the 71 judges who made up that body, had to be present.[26] Moreover, with regard to every particular decision, the ruling of the *Sanhedrin* was based on the votes of the majority.

The contributions of both the *Nasi* and the *Sanhedrin* are both necessary. May we soon witness the reinstatement of both with the fulfillment of the prophecy:[27] "And I will return your judges as in former times, and your advisers as at the beginning," with the coming of *Mashiach,* the ultimate *Nasi,* and the return of the *Sanhedrin.*[28]

---

26. *Horios* 3b.
27. *Yeshayahu* 1:26.
28. See the commentary of the *Radbaz* and others to *Hilchos Sanhedrin* 4:11 as to whether the return of the *Sanhedrin* will predate the coming of *Mashiach,* or whether *Mashiach* will come first.

OUR HOLIDAYS
IN TORAH LAW

WHY THE *SHOFROS* VERSES ARE RECITED

Adapted from *Likkutei Sichos*, Vol. XXXIV, p. 180ff.

OUR OBLIGATIONS ON ROSH HASHANAH

Our Sages state:[1]

The *[Shofar]* blasts and the blessings of Rosh HaShanah... are [all] required to fulfill one's obligation. What is the rationale?

Rabbah explains: "The Holy One, blessed be He, says: 'Recite before Me on Rosh HaShanah [the verses of] *Malchuyos, Zichronos,* and *Shofros: Malchuyos,* so that you will make Me king over you, *Zichronos,* so that the remembrance of you will arise before Me for good.'

How will this be accomplished? With the *Shofar.*"

---

1. *Rosh HaShanah* 34b.

There is a difference of opinion between *Rashi* and *Tosafos*[2] with regard to the statement: "The *[Shofar]* blasts and the blessings of Rosh HaShanah... are [all] required to fulfill one's obligation." *Rashi* interprets our Sages as saying that all of the *Shofar* blasts and all of the blessings are required, and if a person recites the blessings of *Malchuyos, Zichronos,* and *Shofros,* but does not sound the *Shofar,* or sounds the *Shofar,* but does not recite the three blessings, he does not fulfill any of his obligations.

Tosafos,[3] by contrast, maintains that the intent is that all the different *Shofar* blasts are required to fulfill one's obligation; one must sound all the *tekiyos, shevarim,* and the *teruos.* Similarly, all the blessings are required; reciting any one (or two) of the *Malchuyos, Zichronos,* and *Shofros* is of no consequence. But a person's inability to recite the blessings does not detract from his sounding of the *Shofar,* nor does his inability to sound the *Shofar,* detract from his recitation of the blessings.

DEFINING THE ACTIVE AGENT The difference between these two approaches can be explained on the basis of the *Ritva's* interpretation of this *Talmudic* passage. The *Ritva* explains that the question and the response: "How will this be accomplished? With the *Shofar,*" refers to both our coronation of G-d as King, and causing Him to remember us positively. These objectives are achieved by sounding the *Shofar* after the blessings of *Malchuyos* and *Zichronos.*

---

2.   We find the same difference of opinion between the *Rambam* and the *Raavad.* The *Rambam (Mishneh Torah, Hilchos Shofar,* the conclusion of ch. 3) follows the approach of *Tosafos,* while the *Raavad* follows that of *Rashi.*

3.   Whose opinion is also followed by Rabbeinu Asher and Rabbeinu Nissim, and accepted as *halachah* by the *Tur* and the *Shulchan Aruch (Orach Chayim* 593:2), and the *Shulchan Aruch HaRav* 593:4.

The *Ritva* then notes that according to this interpretation, a reason has not been provided for the recitation of the verses of *Shofros,* and offers two explanations:

a) "There is no need [to explain why the verses of *Shofros* are recited]. It is obvious that since [one is sounding] the *Shofar,* the verses of *Shofros* should also be recited."

b) "The phrase 'How will this be accomplished? With the *Shofar'* refers to the verses of *Shofros....* Even a person who does not possess a *Shofar* should mention [these verses] and affirm [them with] a blessing. This is reflected in the wording of the *Tosefta: 'Shofros* so that your prayers will ascend like a *Shofar* blast,' i.e., the intent is the recollection of the sounding of the *Shofar* in prayer." According to this explanation, the recitation of the verses of *Shofros,* and not the actual sounding of the *Shofar,* serves as the catalyst to bring to fruition the purposes of *Malchuyos* and *Zichronos.*

To apply these concepts to the difference of opinion between *Rashi* and *Tosafos: Rashi* follows the first interpretation mentioned by the *Ritva* which puts the emphasis on the *Shofar* blasts as the catalysts that bring to fruition the purposes of *Malchuyos* and *Zichronos.* For this reason, he sees the *Shofar* blasts and the blessings as integrally related one to each other. Thus to fulfill one's obligation, one must sound all the *Shofar* blasts and recite all of the blessings; if any one blast or blessing is lacking, the entire sequence is flawed.

Tosafos, by contrast, follows the second interpretation and understands the *Beraisa* quoted by Rabbah as referring only to the verses of *Shofros.* Therefore all three blessings are considered as a single unit,[4] but there is no integral connection between the blessings and the *Shofar* blasts.

THE PURPOSE OF THE The differences in the
ROSH HASHANAH approaches of *Rashi* and
BLESSINGS *Tosafos* can be appreciated
as stemming from a more fundamental difference: their conception of the purpose of reciting the verses of *Malchuyos, Zichronos,* and *Shofros.* There are two explanations for this purpose:

a) The recitation of these verses brings about G-d's Kingship and His positive remembrance of the virtues of the Jewish people. Just as "Whoever occupies themselves with the study of the laws of the burnt offering is considered as if he brought a burnt offering,"[5] by mentioning the verses of G-d's Kingship, we make Him King as it were. Alternatively, based on our Sages' statement:[6] "The Holy One, blessed be He, Himself observes what is written in His Torah," by mentioning that the Torah describes Him as a King and as favorably remembering the Jewish people, we compel Him to do so, as it were.

b) G-d's Kingship and His positive remembrance of the virtues of the Jewish people are brought about through the prayers we recite. The mention of the verses from the *Tanach* is intended merely to reinforce these activities.[7]

One of the differences between these two explanations is the interpretation of the verses of *Shofros.* According to the first explanation, it is clear that the verses of *Shofros*

---

4. Rabbi Yonason of Lunil explains that the fact that the blessings are considered as a single unit gives us insight with regard to the *Shofar* blasts and teaches us to consider them also as a single unit.
5. End of tractate *Menachos.*
6. *Shmos Rabbah* 30:9.
7. See *Maamarei Admur HaZaken 5564,* p. 217ff.

serve a different purpose than those of *Malchuyos* and *Zichronos*. While the recitation of the verses of *Malchuyos* and *Zichronos* themselves bring about the positive spiritual influences they describe, the verses of *Shofros* are secondary to the actual sounding of the *Shofar*.

According to the second explanation, by contrast, just as the verses of *Malchuyos* and *Zichronos* reinforce the positive effects aroused by our prayers, so too, the verses of *Shofros* reinforce the positive effects aroused by the sounding of the *Shofar*.

Thus according to the first explanation, the question and the response of the *Beraisa:* "How will this be accomplished? With the *Shofar*," does not refer to the verses of *Shofros*, but rather as explained above according to *Rashi's* approach, the sounding of the *Shofar* itself. According to the second approach, by contrast, there is no difference between the verses of *Shofros* and the verses of *Malchuyos* and *Zichronos*. All three sets of verses serve to reinforce the positive influences aroused by the Divine service of the Jewish people.

According to this explanation, the question and response: "How will this be accomplished? With the *Shofar*," refers to the sounding of the *Shofar*. Nevertheless, it provides a rationale for the recitation of the verses of *Shofros* — as explained above with regard to the approach of *Tosafos*, because the intent of the recitation of all the verses is to reinforce the effects of our Divine service by quoting verses from the *Tanach*.

THE POWER OF THE TORAH'S VERSES   A different perspective, however, is evident from the *Tosefta*. Like the *Beraisa* cited above, the *Tosefta* states: "Recite before Me on Rosh Ha-Shanah [the verses of] *Malchuyos, Zichronos,* and *Shofros*," but unlike the *Beraisa,* it mentions also the *Shofros* blessings, stating: *"Shofros* so that your prayers will ascend like a *Shofar* blast," which focuses on "the recollection of the sounding of the *Shofar* in prayer." Thus according to the *Tosefta,* the question and response: "How will this be accomplished? With the *Shofar,"* refers to the recitation of the verses of *Shofros,* indicating that the verses of *Shofros* have an effect beyond that of the *Shofar* itself.

According to the explanation in the previous section, the verses of *Shofros* reinforce the influence of the *Shofar* itself. This follows the pattern indicated by the phrase[8] "And Torah is light," that the Torah causes the influences of the *mitzvos* to be revealed on this material plane.[9] According to the *Tosefta,* however, the verses of *Shofros* have an independent effect. Indeed, the words of the Torah (the verses of *Shofros*) have a more comprehensive influence than the observance of the *mitzvos* (the actual sounding of the *Shofar*).[10]

This concept applies in particular with regard to the verses of *Shofros* which, as explained in *Chassidus,*[11] foreshadow and anticipate the ultimate revelation of the Era of the Redemption, when G-d will "sound the great *Shofar,* and those who are lost in the land of Ashur, and those who were dispersed in the land of Egypt, will bow down to G-d on the holy mountain in Jerusalem."[12]

---

8.   *Mishlei* 6:23.

9.   *Sefer HaMaamarim 5699,* p. 27ff.; *Maamarei Admur HaZaken, loc. cit.*

10. Moreover, there are times — when Rosh HaShanah falls on *Shabbos* — when the influence of the verses of *Shofros* exists entirely independent of the influence of the sounding of the *Shofar,* for the *Shofar* is not sounded at all.

11. See the series of *maamarim* entitled *Yom Tov Shel Rosh HaShanah 5666,* p. 547. See also the *Shiltei Gibborim* to *Rosh HaShanah* 16a which also associates the *Shofros* blessings with the era of *Mashiach.*

12. *Yeshayahu* 27:13, quoted in the *Shofros* blessing, *Siddur Tehillat HaShem,* p. 293.

INSPIRING ATONEMENT

Adapted from *Likkutei Sichos,* Vol. XXVII, p. 124ff.

UNDERSTANDING A PASSAGE FROM THE RAMBAM

In his *Hilchos Teshuvah,* the *Rambam* writes:[1]

2. ...The goat sent to *Azazel* atones for all the transgressions in the Torah, the severe and the lighter [sins]; those violated intentionally and those violated inadvertently.... All are atoned for by the goat sent to *Azazel.*

[This applies] provided [a person] repents. If he does not repent, the goat atones only for lighter [sins].

Which are light sins and which are severe ones? The severe sins are those for which one is liable for execution by a court or *kares*[2].... [The violation of]

---

1. *Mishneh Torah, Hilchos Teshuvah* 1:2-3.
2. Premature death at the hand of G-d *(Moed Kattan* 28a), and also a spiritual punishment that results from the soul's being "cut off" *(Rambam, loc. cit.* 8:1).

the other negative commandments and [the failure to perform] positive commandments that are not punishable by *kares* are considered light [sins].

3. In the present era, when the *Beis HaMikdash* is not standing, and there is no altar of atonement, there remains nothing else but *teshuvah*.

Teshuvah atones for all sins.... And the essence of Yom Kippur atones for those who repent, as it is written:[3] "This day will atone for you."

This passage raises several conceptual difficulties. Among them:

a) There is a difference of opinion[4] between Rabbi Yehudah *HaNasi* and the Sages whether the atonement brought about by Yom Kippur requires *teshuvah* or not. Rabbi Yehudah *HaNasi* maintains that the essence of the day brings atonement whether or not a person repents, while the Sages maintain that atonement cannot be accomplished without *teshuvah*.[5]

Our Sages[4] explain that the same difference of opinion also applies with regard to the goat sent to *Azazel*. Rabbi Yehudah *HaNasi* maintains that its influence generates atonement whether or not a person repents, while the Sages maintain that *teshuvah* is necessary for the atonement to be granted.

---

3. *Vayikra* 16:30.
4. See *Shavuos* 12b-13a; *Yoma* 85b.
5. Even according to the Sages' opinion, the intent is that, as Rabbi Yehudah *HaNasi* explains, "the essence of the day brings atonement." Nevertheless, the Sages maintain that for the atonement generated by "the essence of the day" to effect a person, he must open himself to its influence through *teshuvah*. See the essay entitled "At One With G-d," *Timeless Patterns in Time,* Vol. I, p. 47.

Since the *Rambam* follows our Sages' opinion and maintains that *teshuvah* is necessary with regard to the influence of Yom Kippur, his statements regarding the goat sent to *Azazel* require explanation.[6] "For it appears that, according to the Sages, for some sins, the influence of the goat is effective, even though the person did not repent.[7] Why then does the *Rambam* deviate from our Sages' opinion with regard to these sins?" And why does the *Rambam* make a distinction between the influence of the goat and that of Yom Kippur itself?

b) The *Rambam* states: "In the present era,... there remains nothing else but *teshuvah*." He then continues, stating: "And the essence of Yom Kippur atones," implying that even in the present era, there is still one influence — Yom Kippur — aside from *teshuvah* which brings about atonement.

It is possible to explain that the phrase "There remains nothing else but *teshuvah*" refers to other activities which man can perform. This is indicated by the phrase "and there is no altar of atonement." In the previous generations, there were sacrifices brought by the individual and

---

6. See the glosses of the *Kessef Mishneh* and the *Lechem Mishneh*.

7. The *Meiri (Chibur HaTeshuvah, Maishiv Nefesh, maamar* 2, sec. 13) explains that the intent is that the offering of the goat inspired the person to a limited arousal toward *teshuvah*, but not to a complete commitment. Hence, it is sufficient to atone for his lighter sins, but not for his severe sins.

This explanation is consistent with the *Meiri's* approach that the goat and Yom Kippur itself are merely inspirational influences while *teshuvah* is the actual force that brings about atonement. It does not, however, correlate entirely with the *Rambam's* statements which place emphasis on the power of the goat and Yom Kippur themselves to bring atonement.

the community which brought about atonement,[8] and at present the only action which man can perform to achieve that purpose is *teshuvah*. Yom Kippur's influence, by contrast, is not dependent on man's efforts, and therefore mention of it does not represent a contradiction to the statement: "There remains nothing else but *teshuvah*." Nevertheless, the wording "There remains nothing else but *teshuvah*" is absolute, indicating that there is a dimension of atonement which is solely dependent on *teshuvah*; it is not brought about by Yom Kippur.

c) With regard to the goat, the *Rambam* states: "All are atoned for by the goat sent to *Azazel*. [This applies] provided [the person] repents." With regard to Yom Kippur, by contrast, he chooses the expression: "And the essence of Yom Kippur atones for those who repent." What is the explanation for this change in wording?

A MAN AND HIS DEEDS   The second and third points mentioned above can be explained as follows: In the first *halachah* cited, the *Rambam* speaks of atonement for sins, i.e., that the sin itself becomes washed away. This is reflected in the Torah's description of the atonement brought about by goat sent to *Azazel*:[9] "And the goat will bear upon itself all the sins of Israel." In the present era, "when... there is no altar of atonement," that type of atonement can be gained only through *teshuvah*.

When, by contrast, the *Rambam* states: "The essence of Yom Kippur atones for those who repent," he is

---

8.   Similarly, the punishments of lashes and execution imposed by the court brought about atonement (see *Makkos* 23a). And these punishments are no longer administered in the present era.

9.   *Vayikra* 16:22.

speaking of another form of atonement: that G-d forgives a person for the sins he committed, but the effect is not on the sins themselves. The person is granted atonement, but his deeds are not.

This concept is also reflected in the Torah which says of Yom Kippur:[10] "This day will atone for you, *to purify you* from all your sins," i.e., the sins remain a negative influence; the person is, however, purified, so that he is no longer affected by them.

To explain the concept using wording frequently used in *yeshivos*: The goat sent to *Azazel* and *teshuvah* bring about a change in the *cheftza,* the substance involved, in this instance, the sins. The influence of Yom Kippur, by contrast, affects only the person involved, the *gavra.*

DIFFERENT FORMS OF *TESHUVAH*   Just as the atonement brought about by the goat and Yom Kippur differ,[11] so too, it follows that the *teshuvah* which must accompany both of these spiritual influences is also different. Since the goat sent to *Azazel* and *teshuvah* atone for the sins themselves, therefore the *teshuvah* must involve regret for the sins one performed; one's attention is focused on the sins themselves.

With regard to the influence of Yom Kippur, the *teshuvah* is more personally oriented. One is not repenting for any — or many — particular sin[s]. Instead, one is con-

---

10. *Ibid.:*30.
11. See the *Tosefta* (the conclusion of *Yoma*), *Tosafos,* and other commentaries to *Shavuos* 13a who discuss the interrelation of these two influences during the era of the *Beis HaMikdash,* when, in addition to the purifying influence Yom Kippur itself brings, the goat was sent to *Azazel.*

cerned with the establishment of an all-encompassing bond with G-d.

This distinction is also alluded to in the *Rambam's* wording in *Hilchos Shegagos*:[12] "Yom Kippur... atones only for those who repent who believe in the atonement [it] brings," i.e., the repentance of Yom Kippur is of a general nature, involving one's faith in the spiritual power of the day.[13] If a person does not summon up this measure of *teshuvah,* he has closed himself off to the influence of Yom Kippur, and it will not have an effect upon him.

THE DIFFERENCE BETWEEN THE GOAT SENT TO *AZAZEL* AND YOM KIPPUR The above explanations lead to a different understanding of the difference of opinion between Rabbi Yehudah *HaNasi* and our Sages mentioned above. Rabbi Yehudah *HaNasi* maintains that Yom Kippur has the power to atone for the sins themselves (the *cheftza*). This is indicated by the wording he uses: "For all *the sins* in the Torah, whether a person repents or not, Yom Kippur brings atonement."

The Sages, by contrast, see Yom Kippur as bringing atonement for the person (the *gavra*), but not for the sins itself. This is also reflected in the wording used by Rabbi Yehudah (who expresses the Sages' position): "Is it possible that Yom Kippur will atone for *those who* repent and *those who* do not repent?... Yom Kippur atones only for *those who* repent."

12. *Mishneh Torah, Hilchos Shegagos* 3:10.
13. The *Rambam* continues: "But those who spurn [the influence of the day,] will not receive atonement." Since the person rejects Yom Kippur's influence and does not open himself to its influence, that influence will not be able to bring atonement for him.

Our Sages state[14] that the goat sent to *Azazel* atones for various sins, implying that the atonement is for the sins themselves (the *cheftza*). Since the goat's influence affects the sins themselves, there is room for a distinction between lighter sins and those which are more severe. With regard to the lighter sins, the influence of the goat itself is sufficient to bring about atonement. But for the more severe sins, the influence of the goat alone is not sufficient, and its power must be enhanced through *teshuvah*.

With regard to the potential of Yom Kippur to bring atonement, by contrast, the intent is not that *teshuvah* contributes to the influence of Yom Kippur and grants it the power to atone for a person's *sins* themselves. Instead, the intent is that Yom Kippur has the potential to endow a person with atonement. Nevertheless, for that atonement to affect the person, he must open himself up to its influence through *teshuvah*.

This distinction is reinforced by the mystic conception of the difference between the goat sent to *Azazel* and Yom Kippur. The goat sent to *Azazel* destroys the "body and soul of the *kelipah*," the evil spiritual consequences of the person's sin.

Yom Kippur, by contrast, lifts a person up above the entire context of sin. It awakens the essence of the soul, the point at which a Jew's soul "clings and cleaves to You... the one people to affirm Your Oneness."[15] At this level, there is no existence outside G-dliness, nor any possibility of separation from Him. The revelation of this level of connection removes the blemishes in the soul which

---

14. *Shavuos* 2b.
15. The *Hosha'anos* prayers, *Siddur Tehillat HaShem*, p. 327.

sin caused, cleansing the soul and revitalizing every dimension of our bond with G-d.[16]

---

16. See the essay entitled "At One With G-d" cited above.

FULFILLING A MITZVAH WITH A BORROWED ARTICLE

Adapted from *Likkutei Sichos*, Vol. XIX, p. 348ff.

YOURS OR MINE? The *Talmud* states:[1]

It has been taught: Rabbi Eliezer declares: "A person cannot fulfill his obligation on the first day of the festival [of Sukkos] with a *lulav* that belongs to a colleague, for it is written:[2] 'And you shall take *for yourselves* on the first day, the fruit of a beautiful tree...,' i.e., [these species must be] your own. So too, a person does not fulfill his obligation [using] a *sukkah* that belongs to a colleague, for it is written:[3] 'You shall celebrate the festival of Sukkos for seven days *for yourselves*,' i.e., [the *sukkah*] must be from your own...."

---

1. *Sukkah* 27b.
2. *Vayikra* 23:40.
3. *Devarim* 16:13.

Our Sages [differ,] saying: "Although a person does not fulfill his obligation on the first day with a *lulav* that belongs to a colleague, he may fulfill his obligation [using] a *sukkah* that belongs to a colleague, for it is written:[4] 'Every citizen of Israel shall dwell in *sukkos.'* This[5] teaches that all of Israel are fit to dwell in a single *sukkah.*"

What concept do our Sages derive from [the phrase] "for yourselves"?[6] They require it to exclude a stolen *[sukkah].* A borrowed *sukkah* [is, however, acceptable, for] it is written: "Every citizen...."

The *halachah* follows the Sages' approach, and thus on the first day, a person does not fulfill his obligation with a borrowed *lulav.*[7] With regard to a *sukkah,* by contrast, a person may fulfill his obligation with a borrowed *sukkah.*[8]

A BORROWED SUKKAH, BUT NOT A BORROWED LULAV

From a simple perspective, the Sages' opinion can be explained as follows: The exegesis of the verse "Every citizen..." comes to teach us that although it is written: "You shall celebrate the festival of Sukkos... for your-

---

4.   *Vayikra* 23:42.
5.   The *Levush* 637:2 explains that this concept is derived as follows: Although the word is read as sukkos, plural, it is written סכת, without a *vav,* which appears as a singular usage, indicating that "Every citizen..." will dwell in one *sukkah.*
6.   For it does not contribute to the literal meaning of the verse, and obviously is included for the purpose of exegesis.
7.   *Rambam, Mishneh Torah, Hilchos Lulav* 8:10; *Tur* and *Shulchan Aruch* (*Orach Chayim* 649:2); *Shulchan Aruch HaRav* 649:1.
8.   *Rambam, Mishneh Torah, Hilchos Sukkah* 5:25; *Tur* and *Shulchan Aruch* (*Orach Chayim* 637:2); *Shulchan Aruch HaRav* 637:3.

selves," the intent is not that one must own the *sukkah*,[9] but rather that a person cannot fulfill his obligation in a stolen *sukkah*.

The *Shulchan Aruch HaRav*, however, offers a different interpretation, stating:[10]

> Although the Torah says: "You shall celebrate the festival of Sukkos... for yourselves," i.e., [the *sukkah*] must be your own, and may not belong to a colleague. Nevertheless, a person may fulfill his obligation with a *sukkah* that is borrowed. For since he enters it with permission, it is considered as his own. "For yourselves," i.e., from your own, is mentioned only to exclude a *sukkah* which was stolen.

The *Shulchan Aruch HaRav*[11] thus explains that a person must own the *sukkah* which he uses to fulfill his obligation. Nevertheless, a person may fulfill his obligation with a *sukkah* that is borrowed, because the *sukkah's* owner allows the borrower to consider it as his own.

The question thus arises: Why can't we use that same logic with regard to a *lulav*? Why is a borrowed *lulav* unacceptable?

TO WHAT DEGREE IS IT MINE? It is possible to explain that there are various levels with regard to defining a person's ownership of an article. With regard to a *lulav,* it is required that the person's ownership be complete and

---

9. See the interpretation the *Minchas Chinuch (mitzvah 325, sec. 9)* offers for *Rashi's (Sukkah, loc. cit.)* approach. This is also the approach of *Tosafos (op. cit.)*.
10. *Shulchan Aruch HaRav* 637:3.
11. Whose ruling is based on the interpretation of the *Levush, loc. cit.*

outright. With regard to a *sukkah,* by contrast, one might say that all that is necessary is that the person have permission to use it; there is no obligation for him to have outright ownership over it.[12]

This interpretation is not, however, reflected by the wording chosen by the *Shulchan Aruch HaRav.* On the contrary, the *Shulchan Aruch HaRav* states:[13]

> *A priori,* a person should not dwell in a *sukkah* standing on land belonging to a colleague, for it is not actually called "his own," and the Torah said: "For yourselves," i.e., from your own. [Such a *sukkah*] does not resemble a *sukkah* that was borrowed... Since [a *sukkah*] was borrowed with [the owner's] permission, it is as if it is actually [the borrower's].

Thus the *Shulchan Aruch HaRav* considers a borrowed *sukkah,* not as a lesser degree of ownership, but rather as actually belonging to the owner. And thus we return to the question: Why is a borrowed *lulav* unacceptable?

UNDERSTANDING ANOTHER PERSON'S INTENT It is possible to explain that the phrase "Every citizen..." is not coming to teach us that a lesser degree of ownership is acceptable, but rather to clarify why a borrowed *sukkah* is considered as if it actually belongs to the owner.

To explain: The *mitzvah* of dwelling in a *sukkah* involves considering the *sukkah* as one's *permanent*

---

12. See *Avnei Miluim* 28:43, *Makor Chayim* 448:9, and the *Chasam Sofer* (*Orach Chayim,* the conclusion of Responsum 180) which offer similar — but not exactly the same — explanations with regard to the requirement that a person own the *sukkah* he uses to fulfill the *mitzvah.*
13. *Shulchan Aruch HaRav* 637:11.

dwelling. Thus when a person lends his *sukkah* to a colleague, he is doing so with the intent that his colleague will regard it as his own in the most complete sense. For it is, for that immediate period, considered as his permanent dwelling. This is the very definition of the *mitzvah,* and it is only with such an intent that the *mitzvah* can be fulfilled. And therefore when a *sukkah* is borrowed with the owner's permission, it is taken for granted that the owner intended to give it to the borrower in a manner that it is "actually his."

With regard to a *lulav,* by contrast, the concept that a person must personally own the four species does not define the *mitzvah* itself. It is a requirement that must be met, but it is not an integral aspect of the *mitzvah.* Therefore, for a borrowed *lulav* to be acceptable on the first day of the holiday, the owner must make a specific stipulation that he is giving it to the recipient as a present to be returned.[14] This is not, in contrast to the law regarding a sukkah, a presumption one may take for granted.

| **TWO APPROACHES TO UNITY** | The difference between the laws applying to a *sukkah* and a *lulav* reflect the spiritual qualities of |

these *mitzvos.* Both *sukkah* and *lulav* emphasize the unity of the Jewish people. The *sukkah,* however, underscores the general nature of that unity, that we share a common spiritual heritage. In essence, no Jew is separate from another Jew. And for this reason, "All of Israel are fit to

---

14. To cite another related instance: A person must own the four-cornered garment he is wearing to fulfill the *mitzvah* of *tzitzis.* If he borrows a garment from a colleague, he is obligated to recite a blessing, because we assume that the person who lent it to him lent it with the intent that he could fulfill the *mitzvah (Shulchan Aruch HaRav* 14:6; see also 14:8 and the *Kuntres Acharon).*

dwell in a single *sukkah*." Extending this theme of one-ness, a borrowed *sukkah* is considered as one's own, because this spiritual unity relates even to one's material possessions. It is only when a person's conduct runs contrary to this pattern, as in the instance of a stolen *sukkah,* when one's deeds create separation, that this motif does not apply.

The *lulav,* by contrast, highlights the unity of our people as each one exists within the context of his individual identity. Each of the four species stands for a different category of Jews, and the *mitzvah* involves bringing them together.[15] Nevertheless, since the emphasis is on every person's individual identity, when using a *lulav* belonging to a colleague, a stipulation must be made that it is being given as a present to be returned.

<hr>

15. See the essay entitled "The Unity of Our People" in *Timeless Patterns in Time,* Vol. I, p. 66, where this concept is explained.

LIGHTS IN TRANSITION:

AN ANALYSIS OF THE RATIONALES FOR INCREASING THE NUMBER OF CANDLES LIT ON CHANUKAH

Adapted from *Likkutei Sichos*, Vol. XX, p. 207ff.

WHAT MOTIVATES THE *MEHADRIN MIN HAMEHADRIN?*

Our Sages taught: The *mitzvah* of Chanukah [entails lighting] one candle [each night] for a person and his household. *Mehadrin* (those who perform the *mitzvah* in a conscientious and splendid manner) [light] one candle [each night] for every member of the household.

[What is the practice of the] *mehadrin min hamehadrin* (those whose performance of the *mitzvah* is considered as conscientious and splendid even when compared to the *mehadrin*)? The School of Shammai maintains that on the first night, eight candles should be lit, and [each night] the number should be reduced. The School of Hillel maintains that on the first night, one candle should be lit, and [each] night the number should be increased....

With regard to [the rationale motivating the opinions of the School of Shammai and the School of Hillel], there is a difference of opinion among two *Amoraim*.... One states that the rationale of the School of Shammai focuses on the days which are yet to be celebrated, while the School of Hillel focuses on the days which have already been celebrated. The other states that the School of Shammai [draws a] parallel to the bulls offered on the holiday of Sukkos [which are reduced in number each day], while the School of Hillel's rationale follows the maxim: "One should always ascend with regard to holy matters and not descend."[1]

The Aramaic term for the expression translated as, "There is a difference of opinion among two *Amoraim*...," פליגי בה,[2] implies that the disagreement between the two Sages concerns not only a point of theory, the rationale motivating the different perspectives of the School of Shammai and the School of Hillel, but also a difference in practice. Indeed, we find that certain authorities[3] associate the difference of opinion mentioned in the *Talmud,* with a difference of opinion between the *Rambam* and *Tosafos*

---

1. *Shabbos* 21b.
2. Significantly, in the tractate *Sofrim* 20:5, and in the *Sheiltos d'Rav Achai Gaon (Sheilta 26),* one of the earliest post-*Talmudic* texts of Jewish law, the expression פליגי בה does not appear. Similarly, the two opinions are not quoted as contradictory in the *halachic* works of Rabbeinu Yitzchak Alfasi and Rabbeinu Asher.
3. See *HaNosain Imri Shefer* as quoted by the *Birchei Yosef,* the *Pri Chadash,* and the *Gra,* in their glosses to *Shulchan Aruch, Orach Chayim* 671:1.

regarding the number of candles lit by those who are *mehadrin min hamehadrin.*

Tosafos[4] maintains that the *mehadrin min hamehadrin* light only one additional candle each night. They do not follow the practice of the *mehadrin* who add a separate candle for every member of the household. The *Rambam,* by contrast, maintains[5] that every night the *mehadrin min hamehadrin* add a new candle for every member of the household.

It is possible to explain that *Tosafos* considers the first opinion of primary importance. Accordingly, the number of candles lit must reflect the number of days in the holiday. If every member of the household would light a new candle, confusion might ensue, because an onlooker would not be able to determine how many days of the festival had passed.[6] To forewarn the possibility of such a quandary arising, a new light is not added every night for each member of the household.

The *Rambam,* by contrast, places greater emphasis on the principle: "One should always ascend with regard to holy matters...." Accordingly, every night, each member of the household should follow that principle and increase the number of lights he kindles.

IN PRACTICE, AS WELL AS IN THEORY In the Ashkenazic community, the common custom, as recorded by the *Ramah,*[7] is to

---

4. *Shabbos, loc. cit.,* entry *vihamehadrin.*
5. *Mishneh Torah, Hilchos Chanukah* 4:1-2.
6. E.g., if four candles were lit in a household, it would be unclear whether one person was lighting four candles because it was the fourth night of the holiday, or two people were lighting two candles, because it was the second night of the holiday.
7. *Shulchan Aruch, loc. cit.*:2.

follow the *Rambam's* view. It is possible to explain, however, that this determination does not reflect a preference
for either of the perspectives mentioned above.[8] Nevertheless, even according to the custom which the *Ramah*
mentions, there are several differences in practice
resulting from the views of the two *Amoraim.*

To cite an example: For whatever reason, on the second night of Chanukah, a person kindled only one candle.
According to the opinion that the candles commemorate
the number of nights celebrated, on the third night, he
should light three candles. According to the opinion that
the motivating principle is, "One should always ascend...,"
one might presume that on the third night, it is sufficient
to light just two candles, for this also marks an increase of
light.

A second possibility: A person does not have enough
oil or candles to light more than six lights on the eighth
night of Chanukah. He cannot kindle as many lights as
required. Indeed, he cannot even kindle as many lights as
he did the previous night. Therefore, according to the
opinion that the motivating principle is, "One should
always ascend...," there is reason to presume that he
should kindle only one light. For he is unable to adhere to
this principle at all. Not only can he not add light, he is
actually forced to reduce the number of lights he kindles.
Therefore, it would appear that it is appropriate for him to

---

8.   At present, in the Ashkenazic community, the custom is to light the
     Chanukah candles inside the home, and not in the public domain, as
     was the custom in the *Talmudic* era. The concept of *pirsumei nisa,*
     publicizing the Chanukah miracle, thus applies primarily to the mem-
     bers of the household, and not to the passersby in the public domain.
     Accordingly, since the members of the household are aware of the
     number of people who lit candles, the number of candles kindled
     makes known the number of nights the festival has been celebrated
     (Encyclopedia Talmudis, entry Chanukah).

light only one candle, observing the *mitzvah* according to the minimum requirement.

According to the opinion which focuses on the number of nights the holiday was celebrated, by contrast, each night possesses a certain degree of importance. Therefore, even though one is unable to light the full number of candles that the conscientious commitment of *mehadrin min hamehadrin* would require, it is preferable to light the maximum number of candles one can, and thus accentuate the importance of more of the days of the holiday.

AN ABSTRACT DISTINCTION When viewing the difference of opinion between the two *Amoraim* in the abstract, the variance between their views can be seen as a reflection of a question of a greater scope: Is the custom of the *mehadrin min hamehadrin* related to Chanukah *per se*, or is it a reflection of a general thrust of refinement relevant to our Divine service as a whole? Or to use terminology prevalent in *yeshivah* circles, is it a function of the *cheftza* (the article, in this instance, the days of Chanukah) or the *gavra* (the person observing the *mitzvah*)?

To explain: According to the opinion which explains that the difference of opinion between the School of Shammai and the School of Hillel revolves upon "on the days which are yet to be — or which have already been — celebrated," it is the days of the holiday (the *cheftza*) which warrant the addition (or subtraction) of lights. As such, all the candles lit each night are of equal status. There is no difference between the candles lit to mark the additional nights, and those lit to fulfill the fundamental requirement of the *mitzvah*.

According to the opinion that the difference between
the two schools relates to the number of bulls offered on
the holiday of Sukkos or the maxim, "One should always
ascend with regard to holy matters...," by contrast, there is
no direct connection between the need to add (or subtract)
candles and the holiday of Chanukah. Adding the candles
is an obligation incumbent on the person *(gavra)* which
reflects a comprehensive pattern,[9] applicable in other
aspects of observance as well.[10] For that reason, the
additional candles do not have the same status as the one
candle required to fulfill one's obligation. Indeed, our
Rabbis[11] refer to them as *reshus,* "optional."

IN THE PERSONAL SPHERE In the present era, the *halachah* follows
the School of Hillel, and thus each night
of Chanukah is marked by an increase in
light. And as the *Ramah* writes, it is the
common custom for everyone to observe this *mitzvah* on

---

9. Perhaps this serves as an explanation for the details *Rashi* adds in his
    commentary to *Shabbos, loc. cit.* There *Rashi* states:
    "**The bulls offered on the holiday of Sukkos**": which are progres-
    sively reduced as stated in the passage concerning the sacrifices in
    Parshas Pinchas, and
    "**One should always ascend...**": This is derived from a verse in the
    tractate *Menachos,* in the chapter *Shtei HaLechem.*
    Rashi cites these sources to indicate that the emphasis is on com-
    prehensive Torah principles, and not on concepts relevant to
    Chanukah alone.
10. In this context, one can note the distinction between the terms
    mehadrin min hamehadrin used in this context, and an expression
    frequently used in other contexts, *mitzvah min hamuvchar,* the obser-
    vance of a *mitzvah* in the most preferred manner possible. *Mehadrin
    min hamehadrin* refers to the conscientious and splendid manner in
    which *the person observes* a *mitzvah. Mitzvah min hamuvchar,* by con-
    trast, places the emphasis on the *mitzvah,* and not on the person
    observing it.
11. *Darchei Moshe, Orach Chayim* 674:1.

the level of *mehadrin min hamehadrin.* These concepts should inspire our Divine service throughout the year to come. We must constantly seek to increase light, and we should aspire to observe all the *mitzvos* on the level of *mehadrin min hamehadrin.*

This, in turn, will motivate G-d to respond in kind, increasing the revelation of G-dly light within the world, and leading to the age of consummate revelation when we will again kindle the *Menorah* in the *Beis HaMikdash,* celebrating our Redemption.

AN END TO FASTING

Adapted from *Likkutei Sichos,* Vol. XV, p. 413ff.

CELEBRATION RATHER	The *Rambam* concludes his
THAN FASTING	discussion of the laws of
	the commemorative fasts

with the statement:[1]

> In the future, all of these fasts will be nullified in
> the era of *Mashiach*. Moreover, they will become
> festivals and days of rejoicing and celebration, as it
> is written:[2] "So says the L-rd of Hosts: 'The fast of
> the fourth month, the fast of the fifth month, the
> fast of the seventh month, and the fast of the tenth
> month[3] will be [days of] rejoicing and celebration
> and festivals for the House of Judah; and they will
> love truth and peace.'"

The source for the *Rambam's* statement is the *Tosefta,*[4]
but the wording employed by that source is slightly differ-

---

1. *Mishneh Torah,* the conclusion of *Hilchos Taanios.*
2. *Zechariah* 8:19.
3. I.e., the fasts of the Seventeenth of Tammuz, Tishah BeAv, *Tzom
    Gedalia,* and the Tenth of Teves.
4. *Tosefta,* the conclusion of tractate *Taanis.*

ent: "These days will become festivals for Israel in the future as it is written...." The *Rambam's* change of wording thus raises the following questions:

a) Why does the *Rambam* couple his statements, "these fasts will be nullified.... Moreover, they will become festivals," instead of using the concise wording employed by the *Tosefta?*

b) Why does the *Rambam* omit the phrase "for Israel" employed by the *Tosefta?* Seemingly, it is a necessary addition. For the simple meaning of the prooftext employed by the *Rambam* implies an exclusion — that the fast days will become festivals only for "the House of Judah" and not for the other ten tribes. However, in the era of *Mashiach,* the entire Jewish people, even the ten tribes, will celebrate these festivals.[5]

c) What purpose is served by including the conclusion of the prooftext: "And they will love truth and peace"?

SHARING HAPPINESS It can be explained that the resolutions of the second and third questions are inter-related. The *Rambam* mentions "truth and peace" to offset the exclusion implied by the term "the House of Judah."

To explain: There is reason to say that the celebrations on the fast days in this future era should be restricted to "the House of Judah," because it is they who suffered the most difficulty through our extended exile. The ten tribes

---

5. See the *Metzudos David* to *Zechariah, loc. cit.,* which explains that it is only "the House of Judah" which will celebrate these festivals in the Era of the Redemption, for they are the ones to whom the calamities recalled by these fast days occurred, and they are the ones who commemorated them each year.

The *Chasdei David,* commenting on the *Tosefta, loc. cit.,* however, explains that in the Era of the Redemption, the entire Jewish people will celebrate these festivals.

were exiled beyond the Sambation River[6] and remained there untroubled. The "House of Judah," by contrast, has experienced countless travails in its exile. Since it is the experience of the sorrows of exile which make the celebrations of the Redemption greater, one might think that it is only they, and not the other ten tribes, who will celebrate on these days in the Era of the Redemption.

To counter this supposition, the *Rambam* mentions the final clause of the prooftext: "And they will love truth and peace." Because of the peace and unity that will permeate the Jewish people in the Era of the Redemption, the happiness that will be experienced by "the House of Judah" will be shared by the other ten tribes.

FROM TEARS TO JOY The concept that it is the experience of the sorrows of exile which make the celebrations of the Redemption greater enables us to appreciate three dimensions of the commemoration of the fast days in the Era of the Redemption:

a) There will be no need to fast. As our Sages comment[7] on the prooftext quoted above: "If there is peace, there is no fasting." In the everlasting peace of the Era of the Redemption, the fasts will be nullified entirely.[8]

b) The days will become festivals. This is a direct result of the nullification of the sorrows of exile. For departing from a situation of sorrow and difficulty itself leads to joy.

6. *Bereishis Rabbah* 73:6.
7. *Rosh HaShanah* 18b.
8. In contrast, in the era of the Second *Beis HaMikdash*, there was no obligation to fast on these days. Nevertheless, after the destruction of the *Beis HaMikdash*, the fasts were reinstituted *(Rosh HaShanah, loc. cit.)*.

c) The negative dimension of the fast itself will become transformed into good, as it is written:[9] "And I will transform your mourning to happiness, I will comfort you, and I will grant you joy from your sorrow."[10]

FASTING AS A CATALYST The *Rambam* states[11] that "fasting is one of the paths of *teshuvah*." Thus we find parallels to the three concepts stated above with regard to *teshuvah* motivated by love:

a) Through *teshuvah* motivated by love, a sin can be purged entirely.[12]

b) *Teshuvah* motivated by love prompts a person to increase his good deeds more than is necessary to receive atonement for any one particular sin.[13] Not only is the negative dimension of the sin removed, *teshuvah* provides an impetus to good.

c) *Teshuvah* motivated by love transforms one's sins into merits,[14] i.e., not only does *teshuvah* prompt a person to increase his merits as a whole, it also transforms his previous conduct into merit.

Teshuvah is also the catalyst which will bring about the Redemption, as the *Rambam* writes:[15] "The Torah has promised... that Israel will turn to G-d in *teshuvah*, and immediately she will be redeemed." Not only will *teshu-*

---

9. *Yirmeyahu* 31:12.
10. This verse is quoted by the *Tur* as a prooftext for the same concept stated by the *Rambam* at the conclusion of the laws of commemorative fasts. For a comparison between the treatment of this subject in the *Rambam* and the *Tur*, see *Likkutei Sichos*, Vol. XV, p. 414ff.
11. *Mishneh Torah, Hilchos Taanios* 1:2. As he explains later in that source (5:1), the same concept also applies with regard to the commemorative fasts.
12. *Rashi, Yoma* 86a.
13. *Maharsha, Chiddushei Aggadah, Yoma* 86b.
14. *Yoma, op. cit.*
15. *Mishneh Torah, Hilchos Teshuvah* 7:5.

vah lead to the Redemption as a whole, but it will precipitate many of the particular dimensions of the Redemption, including the transformation of the commemorative fasts. Thus the three motifs mentioned with regard to *teshuvah* are reflected in the three positive dimensions of the commemoration of the fast days that will be revealed in the Era of the Redemption.[16]

MAKING THE BITTER SWEET On this basis, we can resolve the first question mentioned above. The *Rambam* mentions both the negation and the transformation of the commemorative fasts, for each represents another dimension of the uniqueness of the Era of the Redemption. By stating that the fasts "will be nullified in the era of *Mashiach*," the *Rambam* emphasizes the first level, the removal of the sorrow for which we are required to fast. As a direct result, we will experience joy, the second of the factors mentioned above. But by mentioning in a second clause that these fasts "will become festivals and days of rejoicing" and by quoting the prooftext which states that "The fast[s]... will be [days of]

---

16. The above also explains the reason for the *Rambam's* inclusion of the concept of the transformation of the commemorative fasts in the *Mishneh Torah*. On the surface, the *Mishneh Torah* is a text of law and not one of philosophy or homily (see the *Rambam's* Introduction). Nor does the *Rambam* necessarily seek a conclusion of a positive nature to all the divisions of the *Mishneh Torah* (see, for example, the conclusion of *Hilchos Eivel*). What then is the *halachah* implied by the statement that the commemorative fasts will be transformed into festivals?

It is possible to explain that since the *Rambam* includes the laws applicable in the Era of the Redemption in the *Mishneh Torah*, he finds it necessary to explain that in that era, these dates will be observed as festivals. From a deeper perspective, however, one can say that the *Rambam's* intent is to inspire a commitment to *teshuvah* powerful enough to transform the negative dimension of the fast days themselves into positive forces.

rejoicing and celebration," the *Rambam* points to the most complete transformation: that the negative dimension of the fast days itself will become a positive influence.[17]

The two clauses in the *Rambam's* expression also relate to a concept of a greater scope. As explained on several occasions,[18] according to the *Rambam,* there will be two periods in the Era of the Redemption:

a) One period of which it is said:[19] "There is no difference between the present era and the era of *Mashiach,* except [Israel's] subjugation to the [gentile] powers." In that era, "there will be no change in the order of creation. Instead, the world will follow according to its pattern";[20] and

b) A second period following the Resurrection of the Dead when the natural order will give way to a miraculous pattern.

It is possible to explain that the first clause cited above, that the fasts will be nullified — and as a natural consequence, they will be characterized by happiness — will be fulfilled in the first period of the Era of the Redemption. In the second period, when all good will reach its fullest expression, the fasts themselves will be transformed into days of celebration. May this take place in the immediate future.

---

17. To emphasize this concept, the *Rambam* chose this prooftext, although it raises certain questions as explained at the outset.
18. See the essay entitled "Two Periods in the Era of the Redemption," in *I Await His Coming* (Kehot, N.Y., 1991) where this concept is explained at length and sources are annotated.
19. *Rambam, Mishneh Torah, Hilchos Melachim* 12:2.
20. *Ibid.,:*1.

SHOULD MORDECHAI HAVE SACRIFICED HIS TORAH STUDY?

Adapted from *Likkutei Sichos,* Vol. XVI, p. 373ff.

FAVORED BY MOST, BUT NOT BY ALL The *Megillah* concludes[1] by describing Mordechai as: "favored by the majority of his brethren, seeking the welfare of his people, and speaking [words of] peace to all his seed." Our Sages infer,[2] however, that these words of praise contain a subtle hint of criticism: He was favored by "the majority of his brethren," but not by all of his brethren. "Some of the *Sanhedrin* disassociated themselves from him," because "he neglected the study of Torah, [not dedicating himself to study] as often as before, and becoming involved with government affairs."[3]

Our Sages continue, stating that with Mordechai's assumption of court responsibilities, his station among the

1. *Esther* 10:3.
2. *Megillah* 16b, quoted by *Rashi* in his commentary to the above verse.
3. *Rashi, Megillah, op. cit.*

Sages declined; originally he was mentioned as fifth in stature among the Sages,[4] and afterwards he was mentioned as the sixth.[5] This leads the Sages to conclude that "the study of the Torah surpasses saving lives."

This passage raises several questions: a) Since "the study of the Torah surpasses saving lives," why was Mordechai demoted only one position? Why wasn't he removed from the *Sanhedrin* entirely?

b) Why didn't Mordechai himself realize his failing and correct his behavior? Moreover, the above-mentioned verse indicates that he was "favored by the majority of his brethren." Although "some of the *Sanhedrin* disassociated themselves from him," the majority of his brethren, the Sages of the *Sanhedrin,* approved of Mordechai's course of action.

These questions lead to the conclusion that Mordechai's conduct was in fact considered desirable by the majority of the Sages, and it was appropriate for him to serve as one of the leading Sages of the *Sanhedrin.*[6] Indeed, even those Sages who disassociated themselves from him did no more than that. They did not censure him, nor did they seek to have him rebuked. They did not maintain that Mordechai's approach was inconsistent with the Torah's ways, they merely sought a different path of Divine service for themselves.

"BLESSED" OR MERELY "PROTECTED"

The motivating principles for these two approaches can be traced to a differ-

---

4. *Ezra* 2:2.
5. *Nechemiah* 7:7.
6. Note the commentary of the *Ben Yehoyada* to the *Megillah loc. cit.,* who offers a similar interpretation.

ence of opinion between the *Babylonian Talmud* and the *Jerusalem Talmud.*[7] The *Babylonian Talmud* states[8] that the pious men of the early generations would spend nine hours every day praying, preparing themselves for this Divine service, and composing themselves afterwards. The Sages ask: Given this commitment of time, "How is their Torah protected, and how is their work conducted" (i.e., how was it possible that in the few short hours left them, they were able to maintain their level of Torah study, and support themselves financially)? And the Sages answer: "Since they were pious, their Torah (knowledge) was protected and their work was blessed."

The *Jerusalem Talmud*[9] raises a similar question and explains: "Since they were pious, their study and their work were endowed with blessing."

The phrase "Their Torah (knowledge) was protected" in the *Babylonian Talmud* indicates that their piety prevented their Torah knowledge from being forgotten.[10] In the brief time they had to study, they could not, however, advance further in the study of the Torah. The phrase used by the *Jerusalem Talmud,* "their study... [was] endowed with blessing," by contrast, implies that they were also able to grow in their knowledge of Torah. Despite the minimal amount of time available to them,

---

7. The connection between this issue (the concern for the communal welfare of the Jewish people as weighed against the study of the Torah) and the passages which follow was made by the Rogatchover Gaon, Rav Yosef Rosen. When asked by the Previous Rebbe to participate in a Rabbinic committee to protect the interests of Russian Jews, he demurred, explaining that his refusal was predicated by the difference of opinion between the passages from the *Babylonian Talmud* and the *Jerusalem Talmud* which follow.

8. *Berachos* 32b.

9. *Berachos* 5:1.

10. *Rashi, Berachos, op. cit.*

"they succeeded in understanding and comprehending ideas immediately, without delay."[11]

Thus there were some Sages who — following the approach of the *Babylonian Talmud* — saw Mordechai's approach as necessary to maintaining the existence of the Jewish people, but as possessing an inherent limitation. It would lead to the preservation of the reservoir of Torah knowledge which he possessed, but not to its expansion. Therefore, they "disassociated themselves from him."

The majority of the Sages — following the approach of the *Jerusalem Talmud* — realized that Mordechai's self-sacrifice in taking on the yoke of court affairs would, like the piety of the Sages mentioned previously, bring blessing to his Torah study and enable him to advance to new frontiers. Therefore they continued to support him. Similarly, Mordechai himself, aware of this dynamic, persevered in his court responsibilities despite the spiritual sacrifice it entailed.

LIGHT AND DARKNESS This difference of opinion between the *Jerusalem Talmud* and the *Babylonian Talmud* is not merely an isolated, specific issue, but points rather to a more encompassing difference in approach between the two *Talmuds*.[12] Our Sages interpret[13] the verse:[14] "He has set me down in dark places," as a reference to the *Babylonian Talmud*, for the *Babylonian Talmud* is characterized by darkness: questions and challenges,[15] arguments and disputes. Solutions are

---

11. *P'nei Moshe* to the *Jerusalem Talmud, op. cit.*
12. See *Shaarei Orah*, p. 44ff.
13. *Sanhedrin* 24a.
14. *Eichah* 3:6.
15. See the *Zohar* III, 124b quoted in *Tanya, Iggeres HaKodesh*, Epistle 26, which states that a question stems from the side of evil.

proposed and rejected in a lengthy process of analysis that can be compared to a person groping in the dark.

The *Jerusalem Talmud,* by contrast, is characterized by light. Concept follows concept in a natural progression. And when questions do arise, they are answered directly without an extensive process of search.

Based on the *Midrash,*[16] it is possible to conclude that the difference between these approaches depends on "spiritual geography." In *Eretz Yisrael,* spiritual truth is more apparent. As such: "No[where] is Torah study comparable to the Torah study of *Eretz Yisrael.*" The spiritual darkness which characterizes Babylonia — and all lands of exile, by contrast, causes the search for truth to be more protracted, and to involve hypotheses which must ultimately be dismissed.[17]

THE EFFECTS OF "SPIRITUAL GEOGRAPHY" To relate these concepts to the issues mentioned above: Since the process of analysis which characterizes the *Babylonian Talmud* is lengthy and involved, it was impossible for the Sages of the *Babylonian Talmud* to conceive of a person progressing in Torah study without devoting a large block of time to this endeavor. Therefore, when considering the Torah study of "the pious men of the early generations," they could not envision the possibility for growth. All they

---

16. *Bereishis Rabbah* 16:4.
17. Nevertheless, when there is a difference of opinion between the *Babylonian Talmud* and the *Jerusalem Talmud,* the *halachah* generally follows the viewpoint of the *Babylonian Talmud,* for its detailed process of analysis, though more prolonged and difficult, and involving hypotheses that must be rejected, ultimately results in a more thorough sifting of the ideas.

could see was that the attainments they had already achieved would be protected because of their piety.

On the other hand, the Sages of the *Jerusalem Talmud,* whose approach to Torah study was more focused and more direct, appreciated the possibility that a person could "succeed in understanding and comprehending ideas immediately, without delay."[10] Accordingly, the study of the pious could be "endowed with blessing"[8] that would enable them to advance to new frontiers, instead of merely protecting the reservoirs of knowledge which they already possessed.

Since, as mentioned above, these two approaches are dependent on the spiritual influence of *Eretz Yisrael,* similar concepts can be explained with regard to Mordechai's involvement in the Persian court at the expense of his occupation with the study of the Torah. At the time of the Purim story, the *Sanhedrin,* the High Court in *Eretz Yisrael,* followed the approach to study which characterized the *Jerusalem Talmud.* Therefore, Mordechai and the majority of the other Sages of his era maintained that it was proper for him to sacrifice his complete involvement in the study of the Torah for the welfare of the Jewish people. They felt that the spiritual influence aroused by his efforts on behalf of his people would "endow his study with blessing" and he would be able to continue to progress in the study of the Torah despite his court duties.

There were at that time, as there were in the subsequent generations,[18] Sages who came from Babylonia and whose pattern of thinking was nurtured in that land.[19]

---

18. E.g., Hillel who came from Babylonia *(Pesachim 66a),* and Rabbi Nosson of Babylonia *(Gittin 65b).*

19. Indeed, many of the *Anshei Knesses HaGedolah* who returned to *Eretz Yisrael* with Ezra from Babylonia had their thinking processes shaped in that land.

Therefore they were unable to conceive of the possibility that Mordechai would grow in Torah study while burdened with the responsibilities placed upon him by Achashverosh. Accordingly, they "disassociated themselves from him" and sought other individuals to serve as spiritual mentors and guides.

GIVING UP GREATNESS FOR OTHERS There is, however, no question that Mordechai's court duties involved a certain dimension of spiritual sacrifice on his part, as reflected in his loss of position in the *Sanhedrin*. Even according to the approach of the *Jerusalem Talmud* which sees the possibility of Divine blessing enabling a person to continue to advance in Torah study despite a small investment of time, there is no question that a constant involvement in Torah study endows a person with a dimension of greatness that cannot be attained through any other endeavor.

In this vein, our Rabbis[20] point to the uniqueness of those "whose Torah is their occupation," who do not interrupt their study of the Torah for any reason whatsoever, for their study crowns them with a singular aura of personal magnitude. For this reason, our Sages say[2] that "the study of the Torah surpasses saving lives," for the dimension of greatness with which the study of Torah endows one is truly unsurpassable. Because he was forced to forego this dimension of personal greatness, Mordechai descended in stature among the Sages. Nevertheless, it was — in the opinion of Mordechai and the majority of the *Sanhedrin* — necessary for him to make

---

20. See *Shabbos* 11a; *Ramah (Orach Chayim* 90:18), *Tur* and *Shulchan Aruch (Orach Chayim* 106:2).

this individual sacrifice for the welfare of the Jewish people at large.[21]

A JUDGE'S DUTY   A slight difficulty still remains: Although Mordechai's court responsibilities did not prevent him from growing in the study of the Torah, and it was acceptable for him to sacrifice the personal greatness he could have attained for the sake of the welfare of the Jewish people, one might still suspect that he should have resigned his position in the *Sanhedrin* because of his court responsibilities. Seemingly, the *Sanhedrin* should be made up of individuals "whose Torah is their occupation." Without discounting the virtue of Mordechai's conduct and the necessity for it, one might presume that it is not befitting for a member of the *Sanhedrin*. On the surface, a member of that august body should have no other concern in life aside from the determination of Torah law.

This approach, however, misconstrues the purpose of the *Sanhedrin*. The purpose of the *Sanhedrin* was not to serve as an authority on Torah law in the abstract, aloof from the people at large. Instead, our Sages counseled[22]

---

21. The reason this sacrifice was necessary is alluded to in *Rashi's* commentary to the opening words of the *Megillah* which interpret the name *Achashverosh* as meaning that "he persevered in his wickedness from the beginning to the end." Because Achashverosh was so wicked, Mordechai had to retain a position of power in the court, lest that wickedness be vented on the Jewish people again.

This enables us to see a connection between the beginning and the conclusion of *Rashi's* commentary to the *Megillah*. Why was Mordechai required to make the personal sacrifice that caused him to be "favored by [only] the majority of his brethren"? Because of the continuing wickedness of Achashverosh.

22. *Tanna d'Bei Eliyahu Rabbah*, ch. 11. Although this text speaks specifically about the era of the *Shoftim*, the intermediate era between the

that the members of the *Sanhedrin* should "gird their loins with bands of steel, lift their robes above their knees, and traverse from city to city... to teach the Jewish people."

Moreover, we find that undertaking such endeavors detracts from the *Sanhedrin's* authority, for a quorum of 23 judges are necessary to render decisions.[23] For certain rulings, e.g., cases of capital punishment, can only be made when the *Sanhedrin* holds court in Jerusalem, next to the *Beis HaMikdash*.[24] Nevertheless, this is the pattern advised by our Sages, to sacrifice the authority of the court, and have the judges travel from city to city to spur the nation to a deeper commitment to the Torah. Following a similar rationale, Mordechai was willing to sacrifice his own position in the *Sanhedrin* for the welfare of our people as a whole.

IN THE PRESENT AS WELL AS IN THE PAST The Baal Shem Tov[25] interpreted the *Mishnah*:[26] "A person who reads the *Megillah* in a non-sequential order *(lemafreia)* does not fulfill his obligation" to mean that a person who considers the Purim saga as merely a chronicle of history without deriving a contemporary lesson does not fulfill his obligation. Instead, the directives to be derived from the *Megillah,* including its final verse, are relevant in all times, and in all places.

A Jewish leader must know that his main concern is not his personal greatness, nor the contributions to Torah

---

entry into *Eretz Yisrael* and the establishment of the monarchy, the principle applies beyond this specific period as well.

23. *Sanhedrin* 37a; Rambam, *Mishneh Torah, Hilchos Sanhedrin* 3:2.
24. *Avodah Zarah* 8b; Rambam, *loc. cit.* 14:11-13.
25. *Kesser Shem Tov, Hosafos* p. 78.
26. *Megillah* 2:1.

study that he can make, but the welfare of the Jewish people as a whole. When a leader commits himself to this goal, he should not be deterred by the fact that "some of the *Sanhedrin* disassociate themselves from him." Instead, he should persevere in his efforts, confident that "since [he is] pious,[27] [his] study and [his] work [will be] endowed with blessing." He will be given Divine assistance to advance the frontiers of Torah study, and his "work," his efforts on behalf of his brethren, will be crowned with success.

❦

---

27. See *Niddah* 17a which states that a pious man is one who burns his nails after cutting them. As explained by *Tosafos,* this implies that he is willing to accept personal harm in order to benefit others.

A FIFTH CUP OF
WINE AT THE SEDER

Adapted from *Likkutei Sichos*, Vol. XXVII, p. 48ff.

FOUR OR FIVE? Before He redeemed the Jewish people from Egypt, G-d promised Moshe:[1] "I will release you from the Egyptian bondage, I will save you from their hard labor, I will redeem you with an outstretched arm..., and I will take you as My nation.... And I will bring you to the land which I swore to your ancestors."

The standard text of the *Jerusalem Talmud*[2] refers to the first four of these promises as "the four promises of redemption" and explains that to recall them, we drink four cups of wine we drink at the *Seder* on Pesach.

There is, however, an alternate version of that text which also considers "I will bring you..." as a promise of redemption, bringing the number to five. And accordingly, that version speaks of drinking five cups of wine.

---

1. *Shmos* 6:6-8.
2. *Pesachim* 10:1.

Similarly, in the *Babylonian Talmud,* although the standard published text mentions only four cups of wine, the version of *Pesachim* 118a possessed by the *Geonim*[3] states: "'On the fifth cup, one should recite the Great *Hallel,'* these are the words of Rabbi Tarfon."

This difference of opinion was perpetuated in later generations. Thus, when outlining the procedure of the *Seder* in the final chapter of *Hilchos Chametz U'Matzah,* the *Rambam* states:[4]

> Afterwards, he washes his hands and recites the Grace After Meals over a third cup [of wine], and drinks it.
>
> Afterwards, he pours out a fourth cup of wine, and completes the *Hallel* over it, reciting upon it the blessing of song... then he recites the blessing *borei pri hagafen,* [and drinks the wine].
>
> Afterwards, he should not taste anything the entire night except water.

In respect for the version of *Pesachim* 118a possessed by the *Geonim,* the *Rambam* continues:

> One may pour a fifth cup and recite the Great *Hallel* over it, i.e., from "Praise G-d, for He is good,"[5] until "By the waters of Babylon."
>
> This cup is not an obligation like the other cups.

DEFINING THE RAMBAM'S CONCEPTION

In his gloss to the *Mishneh Torah,* Rabbeinu Ma-

---

3.   Cited by Rabbeinu Yitzchak Alfasi. The version of the *beraisa* stated in our texts of the *Talmud* is "On the fourth cup,..."
4.   *Mishneh Torah, Hilchos Chametz U'Matzah* 8:10.
5.   *Tehillim,* Psalm 136.

noach states: "From this, one can infer that it is forbidden to drink wine after drinking the four cups. For if one would surmise that it is permitted, why must one recite the Great *Hallel* over [the fifth cup]?

"Instead, implied is that one should not drink [another cup]. But if one desires to drink, one must recite over that cup songs of praise related to the exodus from Egypt, as one recites over the fourth cup. Otherwise, it is forbidden for one to drink."

Rabbeinu Manoach's statements imply that the *Rambam* considers the fifth cup as optional; if a person desires to drink a fifth cup of wine, he must do so under these conditions. It appears, however, that the matter is left totally to the person's own decision.[6]

It is difficult to reconcile such a conception with the wording employed by the *Rambam*: "This cup is not an obligation like the other cups." Implied is that there is an obligation to drink a fifth cup, merely that this obligation is not as powerful as that concerning the other four cups.[7]

| **POURING, BUT NOT DRINKING THE FIFTH CUP** | Upon deeper consideration, the *Rambam's* approach can be appreciated from a careful analysis of his specific wording. When referring to |

---

6. See also the *Tur (Orach Chayim* 481*)* which quotes a question posed to Rav Saadia Gaon: "If one desires to drink a fifth cup...."
7. Rabbeinu Nissim mentions two opinions regarding the fifth cup. According to the second opinion, it is a *mitzvah min hamuvchar,* "the choicest way of observing the *mitzvah,"* to drink five cups, indicating that it is preferable to drink five cups.

    The *Rambam* does not subscribe to the view quoted by Rabbeinu Nissim, for he does not use the expression *mitzvah min hamuvchar.* There is, however, an association between these two conceptions. Note also the *Raavad's* notes to Rabbeinu Yitzchak Alfasi's *Halachos* which state that "it is a *mitzvah"* to follow Rabbi Tarfon's view.

each of the four cups of wine, the *Rambam* mentions specifically, "recit[ing] the blessing *borei pri hagafen* and drink[ing] the cup [of wine]."[8] With regard to the fifth cup, by contrast, he speaks of "pour[ing] the fifth cup and reciting the Great *Hallel* over it" without mentioning the recitation of the blessing or the drinking of the cup of wine. And if one looks again at the wording he uses, it is obvious why. Directly before mentioning the fifth cup, the *Rambam* states: "He should not taste anything the entire night except water." After stating that a person should not drink anything but water after drinking the fourth cup, the *Rambam* would not say that one may drink a fifth cup.

What then *is* the *Rambam* saying? That we may pour a fifth cup, recite the Great *Hallel* over it, and then pour it back without drinking from it. We find parallels in other situations. For example, when one begins a meal on Friday, finishes eating before sunset, but does not recite grace until after sunset, one may recite grace over a cup of wine. It is, however, forbidden to drink from that cup of wine until after *Kiddush* is recited.[9] In this and other instances, we see that significance is granted to prayers recited over wine, even though that wine is not drunk.

| **RABBI TARFON'S RATIONALE** | What is the rationale for such a ruling? It is possible to say that Rabbi Tarfon differs with the |

Sages who require four cups to be drunk. Thus on one hand, it appears that the *halachah* follows the opinion which requires four cups and forbids drinking any more. On the other hand, the fact that the *Talmud* discusses and

---

8. *Hilchos Chametz U'Matzah* 8:1,5, and 10.
9. *Tur* and *Shulchan Aruch (Orach Chayim* 271:6); see also *Mishneh Torah, Hilchos Shabbos* 29:13.

debates Rabbi Tarfon's view indicates that it is given a certain degree of importance.

How then should one conduct himself? Since the majority opinion forbids drinking more than four cups, that opinion is followed, and only four cups are drunk. On the other hand, in deference to Rabbi Tarfon's opinion, a fifth cup is poured, the Great *Hallel* is recited over it, but as stated above, it is not drunk in compliance with the view that drinking it is prohibited.

Alternatively, it can be explained that Rabbi Tarfon himself does not speak of drinking the fifth cup. To refer to the wording in the version of the *Talmud* cited previously: "On the fifth cup, one should recite the Great *Hallel*." No mention is made of drinking it. For there is a distinction between the fifth cup and the other four cups.

Each of the other four cups of wine is connected with a blessing that plays an integral part in the *Seder:* The first cup is associated with the blessing of the *Kiddush.* The second cup is connected with the blessing *asher gealanu,* which concludes the first part of the *Haggadah.* The third cup is connected with the Grace After Meals, and the fourth cup with the blessing of song that concludes the *Haggadah.* The fifth cup, by contrast, even according to Rabbi Tarfon, is not connected with a particular blessing, or any specific phase in the *Seder.* And therefore, it is of a different nature, and it is not drunk.

ELIYAHU'S CUP

There are those[10] who associate the fifth cup with the cup poured for the prophet Eliyahu. They explain that since there is

---

10. *Ta'amei HaMinhagim,* sec. 551, mentions this concept in the name of the Vilna Gaon.

an unresolved Talmudic question regarding the matter, a cup is poured for Eliyahu, regarding whom it is said:[11] "The Tishbite will resolve questions and difficulties," i.e., in the Era of the Redemption, when Eliyahu will resolve all the questions of Jewish law left open throughout the centuries, he will also resolve the questions regarding this cup of wine.

Notwithstanding the cleverness of this interpretation, when a discerning look is taken at this issue, it becomes obvious that the two subjects are distinct in nature. With regard to the fifth cup of wine, the *Shulchan Aruch HaRav*[12] summarizes the different opinions mentioned above, and rules: "From the early generations onward, it has become the universally accepted Jewish custom not to drink wine after [having drunk] four cups.... Others forbid drinking any beverage.... Their words should be heeded unless there is a dire necessity.... [In such an instance,] if no other beverages are available, only wine, a fifth cup [of wine] is permitted to be drunk, provided the Great *Hallel* is recited."

With regard to the cup of Eliyahu, a custom not mentioned by the *Rambam* but rather originated by the Ashkenazic community,[13] the *Shulchan Aruch HaRav* writes:[14] "It is customary in these countries to pour another cup of wine, besides those poured for those attending [the *Seder*]. This is called the cup of Eliyahu the prophet."

From the fact that the two practices are mentioned in separate sections of the *Shulchan Aruch* and in different

---

11. *Tosafos Yom Tov* and of tractate *Edius; Shaloh* 409a.
12. *Shulchan Aruch HaRav* 481, based on the *Ramah*.
13. See the *Haggadah* of the *Maharil*, and the *Chok Yaakov* 480:6.
14. *Shulchan Aruch HaRav* 480:8.

contexts, it would appear that they are discrete entities.[15] This is also reflected by the fact that Ashkenazic practice regards the fifth cup as permitted only in situations of necessity, but in such situations grants this leniency to every individual. The cup of Eliyahu, by contrast, is a universal practice but is not related to any particular individual. Instead, one cup is poured for every household.

THE SOUL OF THE MITZVAH Every practice mandated by *Nigleh,* the revealed tradition of Torah law, has its parallel in *pnimiyus haTorah,* the mystic dimension of the Torah which guides our spiritual development. In general, our Divine service is associated with four levels, corresponding to the four letters of G-d's name י-ה-ו-ה. These spiritual rungs can be achieved by our service. The fifth cup is associated with a fifth level, a transcendent peak that cannot be attained through any mortal initiative. Nevertheless, when a person has consummated the four levels of Divine service that depend on his efforts, he creates a suitable spiritual setting for the revelation of the fifth level.[16] This level is associated with the fifth cup of wine.

---

15. The association of the two practices is also made in the *Haggadah* of the *Maharil.* Nevertheless, according to the *Rambam's* conception, and according to the development of the concepts in the works of the *Halachists,* it is obvious that they are distinct issues.

16. [To quote a like, but not identical concept: We are commanded *(Vayikra 23:16)* to count fifty days of the *Omer.* In practice, we count only forty-nine, the fiftieth day being the holiday of *Shavuos.* In *Chassidus* (see following essay), it is explained that forty-nine equals seven times seven, i.e., it refers to the full range of our seven emotional qualities which are structured as a set of seven, each one including the other. These qualities are within our potential — and hence, we have the responsibility — to refine and elevate. After we have accomplished this endeavor and created a proper setting — the fiftieth level

Since this refers to an advanced rung of spiritual accomplishment, as a whole, this endeavor is above the scope of people in our age of spiritual darkness. Therefore, this practice is not the prevalent custom in the present age.

The cup of Eliyahu, by contrast, has a future orientation. It was instituted as an expression of our faith in the coming of *Mashiach* and Eliyahu's arrival as his herald. This faith is present in every Jew, and indeed is given more powerful expression in the present generation described as *ikvesa diMeshicha,* the age when *Mashiach's* approaching footsteps can be heard. For as we draw closer to the Era of the Redemption, the faith in the coming of *Mashiach* has intensified. As such, the cup of Eliyahu is a universally accepted practice showing our eagerness to hear the herald's announcement that the time of our Redemption has come.

— a sublime peak identified with the fiftieth gate of understanding is revealed from above.]

SEVEN
PERFECT WEEKS

Adapted from *Likkutei Sichos,* Vol. I, p. 270; Vol. VIII,
pp. 54-55; *Likkutei Sichos, Chag HaShavuos,* 5751

| IS A BREACH | We are commanded:[1] "You shall |
| IRREPARABLE? | count... seven perfect weeks." |

There are sages of the post-
Talmudic era[2] who interpret this charge as implying that
the seven weeks must be counted as a single continuum.
If a person fails to count one day, he no longer has the
opportunity to fulfill the *mitzvah* and need not count the
days which follow. Other sages[3] differ and maintain that
the failure to count one day does not disqualify a person,
and he may — and should — continue counting on the
following days.

Generally, it is explained[4] that the first opinion considers the entire Counting of the *Omer* as one single *mitzvah.*
Hence, the failure to count one day prevents one from

---

1. *Vayikra* 23:15.
2. *Halachos Gedolos.*
3. *Maharitz Chayot,* in the name of Rav Hai Gaon.
4. See *Shulchan Aruch HaRav* 489, *et al.*

continuing to fulfill the *mitzvah*. The second opinion, by contrast, maintains that counting each day is a separate *mitzvah*. Therefore, the fact that a person did not fulfill the *mitzvah* one night does not prevent him from fulfilling the *mitzvah* on the nights which follow.

Because of this difference of opinion, the *Shulchan Aruch*[5] rules that — in deference to the opinion that every day is a separate *mitzvah* — if a person fails to count one day, he should continue counting on the days which follow. Nevertheless — in deference to the opinion that in such an instance a person can no longer fulfill the *mitzvah* — the *Shulchan Aruch* rules that he should not recite a blessing before counting. For according to that opinion, he would be reciting the blessing in vain.

A NEW CONCEPTION OF THE MITZVAH   Several questions are raised with regard to the opinion that the Counting of the *Omer* is considered as one single *mitzvah*. (These questions also apply with regard to the decision of the *Shulchan Aruch*.) Among them:

a) If the entire Counting of the *Omer* is considered as one *mitzvah*, why do we recite a blessing every night before counting? Seemingly, we should recite one blessing, either at the beginning of the counting or at its conclusion.

b) Moreover, according to this opinion, it appears that just as missing the counting of one day prevents one from fulfilling the *mitzvah* in the future, it also has a retroactive effect and nullifies the counting of the previous days. If so, how is it possible to recite a blessing before counting the *Omer*? There is the possibility that one will forget to count

---

5.   *Shulchan Aruch, Orach Chayim* 489:8.

in the future and retroactively the blessing recited will be considered a blessing in vain.[6]

These questions lead to the following conclusion: The Counting of the *Omer* involves 49 *mitzvos*. Therefore, a blessing is required every night, and there is no question regarding the retroactive disqualification of one's counting of the previous nights. Nevertheless, if one fails to count the *Omer* one night, one can no longer count in the future. Why? Because the *mitzvah* is to count the days as a collective sum, for example, to count two or three days. And that is not possible if one has not counted the first or the second night.

Indeed, this concept is reflected in the wording used when counting the *Omer*: "one day...," "two days...," "three days...," i.e., a number that includes the previous days, rather than "the first day," "the second day," "the third day." For every day includes the previous days.[7]

| **CHANGES IN STATUS** | Among the ramifications of the above discussion is the following question:[8] |

When a child becomes *Bar Mitzvah,* a servant is freed, or a person converts during the Counting of the *Omer*, may they recite a blessing when counting the remaining days of the *Omer* or not? Before this change in their status, these individuals were not obligated to fulfill this *mitzvah*. According to the opinion that each night is a separate *mitzvah*, they should count the *Omer* on the subsequent nights to fulfill the *mitzvah* incumbent upon them that night. But according to the opinion that the entire

---

6. *Shibolei HaLeket,* sec. 234; *Pri Megadim, Eshel Avraham* 489:13.
7. See *Likkutei Sichos,* Vol. III, p. 996, which explains the spiritual dimensions of this concept.
8 See *Minchas Chinuch, Mitzvah* 306; *Tziyunim LaTorah,* Principle 12, *et al.*

counting is one *mitzvah,* they will never be able to fulfill the *mitzvah.* Since they were not obligated to count the first days, it is impossible for them to count the entire *Omer.*

In deference to the first opinion, they should count the *Omer* on the subsequent days. But seemingly, in deference to the second opinion, a blessing should not be recited.

With regard to a convert, it appears that there is no need for further consideration of the matter. The status attained by a convert is entirely new, as our Sages comment:[9] "A convert is like a new-born baby." From the time he attains this status, he begins a new leaf. As such, when he converts in the midst of the Counting of the *Omer,* even if he counted beforehand, there is no connection between his previous counting and his counting as a Jew. Hence, his Counting of the *Omer* cannot be "perfect."

With regard to a servant and a minor, however, there is room for discussion. Our Sages obligated a minor in the *mitzvah* of *chinuch,* that he be trained in the observance of the *mitzvos.* Included in the scope of this *mitzvah* is the Counting of the *Omer.* Similarly, a servant may fulfill *mitzvos* even though he is not obligated to. Thus questions arise: When a child or a servant has counted the *Omer* before becoming fully obligated to do so, is that counting significant? Can he continue counting the *Omer* with a blessing in the subsequent days on this basis?

DIFFERENCES BETWEEN THE COUNTING OF A MINOR AND THE COUNTING OF A SERVANT

Insight into the resolution of the above questions can be gained on the basis of the following theoretical discussion regarding

---

9.   *Yevamos* 22a.

the *mitzvos* that involve counting, e.g., the Counting of the *Omer*, and the Counting of the *Shemitah* and *Yovel* years. Is the counting of these days or years significant in its own right? Or is the importance of the counting endowed to it by virtue of the *mitzvah* involved?

To apply this concept with regard to the Counting of the *Omer* by a servant: Do we say that the counting itself is significant, and thus when a servant has counted before he was freed, he may continue counting with a blessing? Or do we say that since it is the *mitzvah* which endows the counting with significance, and the servant was not obligated to count before he was freed, the fact that he did count is of no consequence and his weeks cannot be "perfect"?

There is, moreover, a logical basis for the second opinion, for the passage of time is a factor regardless of whether a person marks its passage or not. What makes a person's taking notice of the passage of time unique and distinct? The fact that he is counting as a result of a Divine commandment and not on his own initiative.

With regard to a minor, it is possible to explain that since the minor was obligated to count because of the *mitzvah* of *chinuch,* that obligation confers a measure of significance to the days he counted as a minor. For this counting involves not merely the marking of the days as does the counting of a servant, but also the fulfillment of an obligation. Therefore, he can continue to count with a blessing in the days that follow.

(This interpretation depends on the explanation given above that even the approach which sees the Counting of the *Omer* as one continuum conceives of the counting of each night as a *mitzvah,* but requires that the counting be comprehensive, including all the previous days. For it is

obvious that the counting of the minor after the attainment of majority is of a different nature than his counting
before he attains majority, and the two cannot be considered as elements of a single *mitzvah.*

When, however, we operate under the conception that
every night is a separate *mitzvah,* but the counting must
continue in an unbroken sequence, it is possible to posit
that the minor's counting before attaining majority will
enable him to continue counting with a blessing afterwards. For his counting beforehand is significant enough
to enable him to count the coming days as a collective
sum.)

| **DIFFERENCES BETWEEN** **RABBINIC AND SCRIPTURAL** **COMMANDMENTS** | This conclusion is not, however, a logi-cal imperative. For the *mitzvah* of |

chinuch is not incumbent on the minor himself. Instead, "a
minor is not obligated to observe any of the *mitzvos....* His
father is obligated to train him in their observance... on
the basis of a Rabbinical commandment."[10]

Moreover, there is a fundamental distinction between
Scriptural commandments and Rabbinic commandments.
A Scriptural commandment may affect the *gavra,* the person observing the commandment — a person is obligated
to perform or refrain from a particular activity. Or it may
affect the *cheftza,* the object or time span in which the
commandment is observed — the object itself becomes
forbidden or the timespan becomes consecrated. Accord-

---

10. *Shulchan Aruch HaRav, Hilchos Talmud Torah* 1:1. See *Likkutei Sichos,*
Vol. XVII, p. 232ff., where this subject is discussed.

ing to many opinions,[11] a Rabbinic commandment is
incumbent only on the *gavra,* i.e., our Sages did not have
the power to cause an object itself to be forbidden, they
could only prohibit a person from using it.[12]

According to this distinction, it is possible to say that
the Rabbinic obligation incumbent on the minor's father
does not endow the days counted by the minor with
enough significance for them to be considered as part of a
single continuum with the days he will count after attaining majority.[13]

THE COMMAND ITSELF ENDOWS IMPORTANCE There is, however, a deeper conception of the principle that the
mitzvah endows an object with significance. On this basis, one can
postulate that when either a servant or a minor becomes
obligated in the Counting of the *Omer* in the midst of the
Omer, they may continue counting with a blessing if they
counted beforehand.

---

11. See the Responsa entitled *Tzafnas Paneach* (Jerusalem, 5725), Respon-
    sum 33; *Mefaneach Tzufunos, Kuntres Meah Savaros; Asvan D'Oraisa,*
    sec. 10, *et al.* See *Sichos Acharon Shel Pesach,* 5736, and the following
    farbrengens, where this concept is discussed.
12. See, however, *Tanya,* ch. 8, which states that even foods which are
    forbidden by Rabbinic decree derive their nurture from the three
    impure *kelipos,* indicating — in contrast to the opinion stated above —
    that a Rabbinic commandment has the power to cause an object itself
    to be considered as forbidden.
13. Even according to the opinion, to be explained, that in the present era
    even the counting of the *Omer* by an adult merely fulfills a Rabbinic
    commandment, it is still possible to make the above distinction. For
    there is a distinction between a Rabbinic commandment of a primary
    nature *(chad diRabbanan,* i.e., a decree which the Sages required of an
    adult) and a Rabbinic commandment of a secondary nature *(trei
    diRabbanan,* the obligation the Rabbis placed on a child to fulfill other
    Rabbinic commandments). See *Shulchan Aruch HaRav* 186:3 where
    this subject is discussed.

To explain: The concept that a *mitzvah* endows the object with which the *mitzvah* must be observed with significance applies even before the *mitzvah* is actually observed. To speak in metaphysical terms, there is no entity in this material world which has any significance in its own right. For in relation to G-d, it is said,[14] "Before Him, everything is of no importance." When can a material entity gain a certain measure of importance? When G-d commands that the entity be used in the observance of a *mitzvah*. With the command itself, the entity becomes significant.[15]

Based on this explanation, it is possible to say that the *mitzvah* of the Counting of the *Omer* itself endows the days with significance. And therefore, when a minor or a servant counted these days despite the fact that he was not obligated by a Scriptural commandment, he can continue counting with a blessing. The days are considered part of a single continuum, because of G-d's command.[16]

---

14. *Zohar,* Vol. I, p. 11b.
15. See *Likkutei Sichos,* Vol. XVI, p. 215; Vol. VII, p. 32, which explains related concepts.

    Needless to say, the fulfillment of the command endows the article with a lasting dimension of holiness which did not exist previously. But independent of whether the command is observed or not, the very fact that it was issued, grants importance to the entity with which it is performed.
16. The person must, nevertheless, do his part in echoing this Divine initiative. Therefore, if he fails to count one of the days of the *Omer,* he has broken the continuum, and can no longer count with a blessing.

    The above concepts do not apply to a convert who converted during the counting. He may not recite a blessing even though he counted the days of the *Omer* before he converted. Since conversion causes him to become a totally new entity, "a new child" as it were, there is no connection between his counting of the *Omer* before conversion and his subsequent counting. The two periods of time cannot be considered a single continuum at all.

REACHING THE   Our Rabbis explain that in the pre-
ULTIMATE   sent era, the Counting of the *Omer*
STATUS   is not considered a *mitzvah* as
                    mandated by Scriptural law. It is
only when the *Beis HaMikdash* will be rebuilt and we offer
the *Omer* sacrifice and the two loaves brought on Shavuos
that the counting will again enjoy the status of a Scriptural
commandment.[17]

This is alluded to in the prayer we recite together with
the Counting of the *Omer*:[18] "May the Merciful One restore
the *Beis HaMikdash* to its place, speedily in our days." As
the Alter Rebbe explains:[19] "The only reason we count [the
Omer] in the present era is to commemorate [the practice
of] the *Beis HaMikdash*.... Therefore, we pray that the *Beis
HaMikdash* be speedily rebuilt, and then we will be able to
fulfill the *mitzvah* in its proper manner."

The simple meaning is that we are praying that
Mashiach will come so that next year, we will be able to
fulfill the Counting of the *Omer* in a full and complete
manner. Based on the above, and based on our anticipa-
tion that *Mashiach* will come in the most immediate
future, it can be explained that the prayer expresses our
wish that *Mashiach* come now, and then we will continue
counting the *Omer* this year in fulfillment of a Scriptural
commandment.[20] For like a child who has attained matur-

---

17. *Shulchan Aruch HaRav* 489:2.
18. *Siddur Tehillat HaShem*, p. 341.
19. *Shulchan Aruch HaRav* 489:11.
20. One might raise a difficulty: As evident from the *Shulchan Aruch
    HaRav* 489:2, the Counting of the *Omer* attains the status of a Scrip-
    tural commandment only after the *Omer* has been offered. If *Mashiach*
    will come in the midst of the *Omer*, the *Omer* itself will not have been
    offered, and hence the counting will not have the status of a Scriptural
    mitzvah.

ity in the midst of the Counting of the *Omer*, our counting before *Mashiach's* coming will be considered significant, and will enable us to continue fulfilling the *mitzvah* in the most complete manner, together with *Mashiach* in the *Beis HaMikdash*. May this come to pass in the immediate future.

❧

This difficulty can be resolved as follows: When describing the Counting of the *Omer*, the Torah *(Vayikra* 23:15) states: "You shall count seven weeks from the day after the day of rest, [i.e., the Pesach holiday,] when you brought the *omer* as a wave offering until the day after the seventh week... when you will bring new grain as a meal offering...." The Torah associates the counting with both the *omer* offering and the two loaves of grain on Shavuos. Thus even if the *omer* offering was not brought on the sixteenth of Nissan, the counting can still be considered a Scriptural commandment because of the connection to the offering which will be brought on Shavuos. See the Responsa of the Radbaz, Responsum 1327.

Note sources quoted in *Likkutei Sichos, Chag HaShavuos*, 5751, footnotes 17 and 35.

WHEN SHAVUOS IS
TO BE CELEBRATED

Adapted from *Likkutei Sichos,*
Vol. III, p.995ff.; Vol. IV, p. 1030

A UNIQUE HOLIDAY Shavuos differs from every other Jewish holiday. The Torah mentions the specific dates on which the holidays of Pesach, Sukkos, Rosh HaShanah, and Yom Kippur should be celebrated. With regard to the holiday of Shavuos, by contrast, no date is given. Instead the Torah states:[1]

> You shall count seven perfect weeks... From the day you brought the *omer* as a wave offering... you shall count fifty days. [On that fiftieth day,] you shall present a meal offering of new [grain].... This very day shall be proclaimed as a sacred holiday.

Thus the observance of the holiday of Shavuos is not dependent on a particular day of the month, but on the conclusion of the Counting of the *Omer*. Although at present Shavuos is always celebrated on the sixth of Sivan,

---

1. *Vayikra* 23:15-21.

this is because in the present era, we follow a fixed calendar. In the era when the monthly calendar was established
by the testimony of witnesses with regard to the sighting
of the moon, however, Shavuos, the fiftieth day of the
Omer, could also fall on the fifth of Sivan (if both Nissan
and Iyar were months of 30 days) or on the seventh of
that month (if both Nissan and Iyar were months of 29
days).[2]

The sixth of Sivan is the anniversary of the giving of
the Torah,[3] and our celebration of the holiday commemo-
rates this event. This concept is also echoed in our prayers
which describe the holiday as "the season of the giving of
our Torah."[4] Nevertheless, the Alter Rebbe rules[5] that this
description is appropriate only when the holiday of Shavuos is celebrated on the sixth of Sivan, the anniversary of
the giving of the Torah. In the previous era, when Shavuos
was celebrated on dates other than the sixth of Sivan, it
was not referred to as "the season of the giving of our
Torah."[6]

---

2. *Rosh HaShanah* 6b.
3. For the *halachah* follows the opinion of the Sages and not of Rabbi
   Yossi *(Shabbos* 86b).
   This explanation does not follow the approach of the *Divrei Nechemiah (Hashlamus LiShulchan HaRav,* sec. 581, *Kuntres Acharon),* which
   states that the Torah was given on the seventh of Sivan. This hypothe-
   sis is refuted by the ruling of the *Shulchan Aruch HaRav* 494:1 which
   states that even the Sages maintain that the Jews left Egypt on a
   Thursday. In that year, both Nissan and Iyar contained 30 days. Thus
   although there were 51 days between Pesach and the giving of the
   Torah, the Torah was given on the sixth of Sivan.
4. *Siddur Tehillat HaShem,* pp. 250, 253, 258.
5. *Shulchan Aruch HaRav* 494:1.
6. This ruling differs from the conclusion of the *Divrei Nechemiah (loc.
   cit.),* who maintains that even when Shavuos was observed on a day
   other than the sixth of Sivan, it was referred to as "the season of the
   giving of our Torah," because at that time the fiftieth Gate of Wisdom
   is revealed.

WHEN PAST AND PRESENT MEET The possibility that the holiday of Shavuos will be celebrated on a day other than the sixth of Sivan applies in the present era as well. According to the fixed calendar we follow, Nissan always has 30 days, and Iyar, 29; thus, Shavuos will always fall on the sixth of Sivan. Nevertheless, there are situations in which an individual person is required to celebrate Shavuos on a different date.

To understand this concept, one premise must be established. Based on the phrase,[7] "And you shall count for yourselves...," our Sages emphasize[8] that the *mitzvah* of the Counting of the *Omer* is incumbent on every single person as an individual (in contrast to the Counting of the *Shemitah* and *Yovel*[9] years which are counted by the Jewish court[10]). The Jewish people do not count the *Omer* as a collective entity; instead the reckoning must be individual in nature.

Taking this concept a step further, it follows that the date on which Shavuos is observed is also a personal matter. For as stated above, Shavuos is not associated with any particular date on the calendar, but instead, depends on the completion of the Counting of the *Omer*.[11]

---

7. *Vayikra* 23:15. The word *lechem*, "for yourselves," appears superfluous. Hence, our Sages conclude that it alludes to this concept.
8. *Menachos* 65b; *Shulchan Aruch HaRav* 489:1.
9. Sabbatical and Jubilee.
10. *Rambam, Mishneh Torah, Hilchos Shemitah VeYovel* 10:1.
11. The intent is not that the Counting of the *Omer* (or the obligation to count the *Omer*) brings about the holiday of Shavuos. For even individuals who were not obligated to count the entire *Omer*, for example, a minor who came of age or a person who converted during the Counting of the *Omer*, are obligated to observe the holiday of Shavuos on the fiftieth day after Pesach according to Scriptural law.

    Were the holiday of Shavuos to be totally dependent on the Counting of the *Omer*, the question would arise: How is it possible for

As such, even when a person's Counting of the *Omer* concludes before or after the Counting of the *Omer* of others, it is then that he is required to observe Shavuos.[12] We cannot say that with regard to the Counting of the *Omer*, the person should follow an individual reckoning but with regard to the observance of Shavuos he should observe the holiday with the others around him, for the sole determinant of when Shavuos should be observed is the Counting of the *Omer*. And the Counting of the *Omer* is given over to each individual as an individual, not to the Jewish people as a collective.[13]

---

these individuals to observe Shavuos when they did not count the *Omer* previously?

The explanation that the holiday is brought about by the Counting of the *Omer* by the Jewish people as a whole is unacceptable. For as mentioned above, there is no such concept as the Counting of the *Omer* by the Jewish people as a whole. Our Sages define the Counting of the *Omer* as a *mitzvah* which relates to the individual, and not to the collective.

Therefore, we must conclude that the holiday of Shavuos is not brought about by the Counting of the *Omer*. Instead, the explanation must be that the need to observe the holiday is mandated by Scriptural law, the time when that holiday is observed, however, is determined by the Counting of the *Omer*. And as stated above, the Counting of the *Omer* serves as an indicator on an individual basis; when each person completes his Counting of the *Omer*, on the following day, he observes Shavuos.

12. It is improper to say that, although he counted the 49 days of the *Omer,* since the total of these 49 days did not include (or included more than) 49 times 24 hours, the weeks of the *Omer* are not considered "perfect weeks," and therefore, he should not observe Shavuos at this time. This is evidenced by the fact that all agree that when a person travels from west to east without crossing the dateline, he must begin observing Shavuos as soon as the sun sets after the fifth of Sivan despite the fact that his 49 days of counting the *Omer* did not include 49 times 24 hours.

13. Nevertheless, from the Counting of the *Omer* of the Jews as individuals result certain obligations, e.g., the additional offerings sacrificed on Shavuos, which are incumbent on our people as a collective.

The observance of *Shabbos* and other festivals depends on the local practice as defined by the calendar dates which are determined by the rising and setting of the sun in that locale.[14] Shavuos, by contrast, depends not on the calendar, but on the Counting of the *Omer*, and that is an individual matter.

THE BEAT OF A DIFFERENT DRUM   In previous generations, the above issue was largely theoretical in nature. At present, however, the advances in technology and the dispersion of the Jews throughout the world have made the matter a question of practical relevance.

To explain: Since the earth is shaped like a globe,[15] and the sun (upon whose movement the determination of the days depends) travels across the earth's horizon, there must be a line on the earth (the international dateline) at which the days differ. A person standing on one side of

---

To cite a parallel: Although there are different principles regarding monetary law *(dinei memonos)* and laws regarding capital punishment *(dinei nefashos)*, at times a decision regarding monetary law will have repercussions with regard to the laws regarding capital punishment, and vice versa.

14. There is a slight question with regard to the Seventh Day of Pesach and Shemini Atzeres, for the observance of these holidays is generally not associated with a specific date (although *Shmos* 12:18 mentions the date of the Seventh Day of Pesach), but rather is determined by the first day of Pesach, and the first day of the holiday of Sukkos.

There is, however, a distinction between these holidays and Shavuos. For as mentioned, the Counting of the *Omer*, on which Shavuos depends, is an individual manner, and its seven weeks must be "perfect." With regard to these holidays, by contrast, the obligation is to observe the seventh day or the eighth day of the festival as it is observed in one's immediate locale. The fact that by doing so, one will have skipped a day of the holiday is not significant. See *Likkutei Sichos,* Vol. VII, p. 287.

15. The *Jerusalem Talmud (Avodah Zarah* 3:1, cited by *Tosafos, Avodah Zarah* 41a); *Bamidbar Rabbah* 13:14; *Zohar,* Vol. III, p. 10a.

that line is in the midst of a different day than the person on the other side of the line. By crossing that line, a person skips a day, as it were. Thus if a person goes from east to west, he will proceed from Sunday to Tuesday, skipping Monday. Conversely, when a person goes from west to east, moving opposite to the sun's pattern, he will repeat a day, e.g., he will have two Sundays.

Ordinarily, these concepts do not affect our ritual observance. With regard to the Counting of the *Omer,* however, the crossing of the dateline makes a significant difference. As mentioned above, the counting of the *Omer* is a *mitzvah* which is dependent on every person as an individual. Thus when a person crosses the dateline in the middle of counting the *Omer,* he must continue according to his own personal reckoning although everyone around him is counting a different day.

For example, Pesach falls on *Shabbos.* On Monday, the second day of the Counting of the *Omer*, a person travels from east to west [e.g., from the U.S. to Australia]. Although he left on Monday, when he crosses the dateline, it will be Tuesday. That night [the night between Tuesday and Wednesday], he is required to count the third day of the *Omer,* while the local people will be counting the fourth day.

Conversely, if a person crosses the dateline while traveling from west to east, leaving Monday and arriving on Monday, on the night between Monday and Tuesday, he must count the third day of the *Omer,* although the local people will be counting the second day.

CELEBRATING SHAVUOS ON A DIFFERENT DAY THAN EVERYONE ELSE As mentioned above, the holiday of Shavuos is not dependent on a particular day of the month, but on the conclusion of the Counting of the *Omer,* and, moreover, that reckoning is individual in nature. Accordingly, when someone crosses the dateline from west to east, the fifth of Sivan is the fiftieth day of his Counting of the *Omer.* He must observe Shavuos on that day with regard to all matters except the reference to the holiday as "the season of the giving of our Torah."[16] If he lives in the diaspora, he should observe the sixth of Sivan as the second day of the holiday.

Conversely, if someone crosses the dateline from east to west, he should observe Shavuos on the seventh of Sivan. If he lives in the diaspora, he should observe the eighth of Sivan as the second day of the holiday.

THE SECOND DAY IS ALSO DIFFERENT The concept that the observance of Shavuos depends on the conclusion of the Counting of the *Omer* and not on a particular calendar date also has ramifications with regard to the second day of the holiday. With regard to the holidays of Pesach and Sukkos (both the first and last days), in the era when the sanctification of the moon was established according to the testimony of witnesses, the observance of a second day was instituted in the outlying areas of the diaspora[17] because of a doubt concerning the day on which the holiday was to be observed. If messengers from Jerusalem were not able to

---

16. For, as above, that is only appropriate when Shavuos is observed on the sixth of Sivan.
17. See *Rambam, loc. cit.* 3:11, 5:9-12.

reach these communities and inform them when the new moon had been consecrated, they would have to observe the holidays for two days, because they did not know which day was the fifteenth of the month. Even after the new moon was no longer sanctified on the basis of the testimony of witnesses, and instead, a fixed calendar was adopted, these communities continued observing the second day of the festivals in respect for the custom practiced by their ancestors.[18]

The above concepts do not apply with regard to the holiday of Shavuos. Since the observance of the holiday is not associated with a particular day of the month, but is instead dependent on the Counting of the *Omer,* there was never any doubt regarding the day of its observance. Even in the era when the new moon was consecrated according to the testimony of witnesses, by the sixth of Sivan, the Jews living in the most distant diaspora had been informed when the month of Nissan had been consecrated, and thus when Pesach and the Counting of the *Omer* had begun.

Why then was Shavuos observed for two days? In order not to make a distinction between one festival and another.[19] Were the second day of this festival not to be observed in the diaspora, the Jews living there might have treated the observance of the second day of other festivals lightly. To prevent that from happening, our Sages ordained that the second day of Shavuos be observed as a

---

18. *Beitzah* 4b; *Rambam, op. cit.* 5:5.
      At present, because we follow a fixed calendar, there is no doubt concerning the day on which these holidays are to be observed. Nevertheless, there are still certain leniencies that are followed because originally, these days were instituted because of a doubt. See *Shulchan Aruch, Orach Chayim* 393:1, 527:22.
19. See *Rambam, loc. cit.* 3:12.

festival, despite the fact that there was never a doubt regarding the day the holiday was to be observed.

This conveys a more severe status upon the second day of Shavuos than that of the second day of other festivals. For as mentioned above, the observance of the second day of other festivals is associated with doubt, while the observance of the second day of Shavuos is a decree of our Sages regarding which doubt never existed.[20]

THE SPIRITUAL DIMENSION OF THE SEQUENCE The connection between the individual nature of the Counting of the *Omer* and Shavuos has ramifications with regard to the inner dimensions of our Divine service. The Divine service appropriate for the Counting of the *Omer* is the refinement of our emotional qualities. We count seven weeks corresponding to the seven emotional qualities, and 49 days (7x7), for each of these qualities is interrelated with the others. The objective is to make these weeks — and the corresponding emotional qualities — "perfect."

When a Jew finishes the refinement of his emotional qualities, he is granted the Torah as a gift from above. This is totally dependent on him; it makes no difference what is happening with the people around him. When he has refined his 49 emotional qualities, he is granted the Torah, the fiftieth Gate of Knowledge, even though the others around him may not have reached that degree of preparation.

Conversely, if his personal process of refinement is slower and he has not refined his emotional characteris-

---

20. See the Responsa of the *Chasam Sofer, Orach Chayim,* Responsum 145, which establishes an equivalence between the second day of Shavuos and the second day of Rosh HaShanah.

tics, he must wait until he has completed his task of refinement, although those around him are being granted the Torah.

THE FAST OF
THE FOURTH MONTH

Adapted from *Likkutei Sichos*, Vol. XVIII, pp. 308-309

WHY WE FAST ON	The *Rambam* states:[1]
THE SEVENTEENTH	There are days when the
OF TAMMUZ	entire Jewish people fast

because of the calamities that occurred on those dates, to arouse their hearts and inspire them to the paths of *teshuvah*.

The *Rambam* continues,[2] mentioning the four dates on which fasts were instituted because of the destruction of Jerusalem and the *Beis HaMikdash:* the third of Tishrei, the tenth of Teves, the seventeenth of Tammuz, and the ninth of Av. He explains[3] that these fasts are specifically mentioned in the prophetic tradition, for Zechariah refers[4] to "the fast of the fourth month [i.e., Tammuz], the fast of the fifth month [Av], the fast of the seventh month

---

1. *Mishneh Torah, Hilchos Taanios* 5:1.
2. *Ibid.:2-3.*
3. *Ibid.:4.*
4. *Zechariah* 8:19.

[Tishrei], and the fast of the tenth month [Teves]," indicating that the practice of fasting was not ordained by the Sages after the destruction of the Second *Beis HaMikdash*, but was observed in Babylon after the destruction of the First *Beis HaMikdash*. Even after the return of the people to *Eretz Yisrael*, these fasts were still observed.[5]

With regard to the seventeenth of Tammuz, the *Rambam*[6] mentions five reasons for the fast:

a) The tablets [of the Ten Commandments] were broken;

b) In the era of the First *Beis HaMikdash*, the offering of the daily sacrifice ceased;

c) In [the war leading to] the destruction of the Second *Beis HaMikdash*, the walls of Jerusalem were breached;

d) Apostumus, the wicked, burnt a Torah scroll,

e) and he[7] erected an idol in the Sanctuary.

With this wording, the *Rambam* reconciles a difficulty in the words of our Sages. The *Jerusalem Talmud*[8] and other sources[9] interpret the phrase "the fast of the fourth month" in Zechariah's prophecy as referring to the seventeenth of Tammuz on which "[the walls of] the city were breached." Since Zechariah was speaking before the destruction of the Second *Beis HaMikdash,* it would appear that the *Jerusalem Talmud* is implying that the walls of the

---

5. See *Rosh HaShanah* 18b which describes the manner in which these fast days were observed.
6. Interpreting the *Mishnah, Taanis* 4:6.
7. I.e., Apostumus, a Greek official in the era of the Second *Beis HaMikdash*. Others interpret this as a reference to the idol erected by King Menashe in the era of the First *Beis HaMikdash (Jerusalem Talmud, Taanis 4:6)*.
8. *Ibid.*
9. *Sifri* 6:4; *Tosefta, Sotah,* the conclusion of ch. 6. Some authorities also accept this as the correct version of the text in the *Babylonian Talmud, Rosh HaShanah, loc. cit.*

city were breached in its destruction by the Babylonians on the seventeenth of Tammuz. This contradicts explicit statements in the Book of *Yirmeyahu*[10] which state that the walls of the city were destroyed by the Babylonians on the ninth of Tammuz.

From the *Rambam's* wording, we can explain why the fast is commemorated on the seventeenth of Tammuz despite the fact that the walls were breached by the Babylonians on the ninth of that month. Our people were unwilling to accept two communal fasts in one month.[11] Therefore, even during the era of the Second *Beis HaMikdash,* the fast was observed on the seventeenth of Tammuz, and not on the ninth. For the severity of the destruction of the Tablets and the cessation of sacrificial offerings outweighs that of the destruction of the city's walls.[12]

THE NINTH OR THE SEVENTEENTH? The *Jerusalem Talmud*[13] itself recognizes the contradiction from the verses in *Yirmeyahu* and explains: "Confusion exists with regard to the dates." Generally,[14] that statement is interpreted simply: Because of the tremendous travail — both material and spiritual — suffered by the Jewish people at the destruction of Jerusalem and the *Beis HaMikdash,* the people erred in reckoning the dates. Although the walls of the city were

---

10. *Yirmeyahu* 39:2, 52:6-7.
11. *Jerusalem Talmud, loc. cit.*
12. See the gloss *Tzafnas Paneach* to the *Mishneh Torah, loc. cit.*
13. The *Babylonian Talmud (Taanis* 28b, and most versions of *Rosh HaShanah, loc. cit.*), by contrast, follows the simple meaning of the verse which states that the walls of Jerusalem were breached by the Babylonians on the ninth of Tammuz.
14. See the gloss of the *Turei Even, Rosh HaShanah, loc. cit.,* and the *Gevuros Ari* to *Taanis, loc. cit.*

breached on the seventeenth of Tammuz, they thought
that this occurred on the ninth. When the *Tanach*
recorded the matter, it did not desire to deviate from the
popular tradition, and therefore also stated that the walls
were breached on the ninth.

The *Maharsha* offers a different interpretation,[15]
explaining that the *Jerusalem Talmud's* intent is not that
there was an error in calculations, but a difference in
approach. The gentiles follow a solar calendar, and
according to their reckoning, the walls were breached on
the ninth of Tammuz. The Jews, however, follow a lunar
calendar, and according to the lunar calendar, it was on
the seventeenth that the walls were breached.[16]

Based on *Rashi's* commentary on the Book of *Yirmeyahu*, a slightly different interpretation can be offered.
On the verses:[17] "I see a rod of an almond tree. G-d said to
me: 'You have seen well, for I will diligently pursue[18] My
word to perform it,'" *Rashi* explains that just as an almond
tree produces fruit in 21 days, so too, there was a 21-day
interval between the breaching of the city's walls on the
seventeenth of Tammuz, and the destruction of the *Beis
HaMikdash* on the ninth of Av. This prophecy refers to the
destruction of the First *Beis HaMikdash* by the Babylonians.

In order that this interpretation not run contrary to the
verses which describe the walls as being breached on the

---

15. *Chiddushei Aggados, Taanis, loc. cit.*
16. There is an eleven-day difference each year between the lunar calendar and the solar calendar. Thus in the month of Tammuz, the
difference is eight days, the difference between the seventeenth and
the ninth *(ibid.).*
17. *Yirmeyahu* 1:11-12.
18. The Hebrew term for "diligently pursue," *shokaid,* shares the same
root as the Hebrew for almond tree, *shakaid.*

ninth of Tammuz, we are forced to explain that the city was conquered in stages. On the ninth of Tammuz, the outer wall of Jerusalem was breached, and afterwards, on the seventeenth of Tammuz, the inner wall surrounding the *Beis HaMikdash* fell.

The prophecy of Zechariah mentioned at the outset states that in the future, the communal fasts will be transformed "into holidays and days of celebration." One may infer that according to the severity of the calamity for which we fast, so too, will be the intensity of the joy with which the day is celebrated during the Era of the Redemption.[19] Thus the recurrence of tragedies on the seventeenth of Tammuz indicates that ultimately it will be revealed as a great festival. May this take place in the immediate future.

---

19. See the essay entitled "Support for Jerusalem," *Timeless Patterns in Time,* Vol. I, p. 135 where this concept is explained.

Unlocking the Aggadah

OF ETERNAL LIFE

Likkutei Sichos, Shabbos Parshas Vayechi, 5751;
from the *Sichos* of 20 Menachem Av, 5731

I. Our Sages relate:[1]

Rav Nachman and Rav Yitzchak were sitting together at a repast. Rav Nachman asked Rav Yitzchak: "Share a word [of Torah]."

[Rav Yitzchak] replied: "Rabbi Yochanan taught as follows: One should not speak during a meal lest the windpipe open before the esophagus, causing danger. {When a person speaks, the covering of the windpipe opens, and [it is possible] for food to enter. This would cause danger.... [Generally,] food and drink pass through the esophagus.[2]}

---

1. *Taanis* 5b.
2. *Rashi, Taanis, loc. cit.* As is well known, there is a debate among the authorities if the commentary ascribed to *Rashi* on this tractate was indeed authored by him or not. (See *Maharatz Chayos*, at the conclusion of the tractate of *Taanis, Shem HaGedolim*, from the *Chidah*, entry *Rashi*.)

After [Rav Yitzchak] finished eating,[3] he told him: "Rabbi Yochanan said the following: Yaakov Avinu did not die, (rather, he lives forever)."[4]

[Rav Nachman] replied to him: "Was it for naught that he was mourned, embalmed, and buried?"[5]

[Rav Yitzchak] told him: "My statements are based on a verse. It is written:[6] '"Do not fear, My servant Yaakov," speaks G-d, "And do not dismay, O Israel. For I will deliver you from afar, and your descendants from the land of their captivity."' An association is established between [Yaakov] and his descendants. Just as his descendants are alive, he too is alive."

The commentaries[7] have noted several difficulties with this passage. [Among them:]

a) What did Rav Yitzchak gain by saying: "One should not speak during a meal..."? Seemingly, mentioning this directive itself is also a contradiction to its instructions.[8] On the contrary, the concept "Yaakov Avinu did not die"

---

3. This is the version quoted by the *Ein Yaakov*. Our texts of the Talmud state, "After they finished eating," which indicates that they were both eating. According to the version of the *Ein Yaakov*, it might appear that Rav Yitzchak had already finished eating previously. See note 29 below.

4. *Tosafos (Taanis, loc. cit.)* derives this concept from the exegesis of *Bereishis* 49:33 which uses the word ויגוע for "and he died," rather than the more common וימת, as explained in *Sotah* (13a) with regard to Chushim. See also a similar interpretation in *Rashi's* commentary on the Torah.

5. *Bereishis* 50:2, 10, 13.

6. *Yirmeyahu* 30:10.

7. Note the commentaries to the *Ein Yaakov*.

8. Indeed, we find that mentioning the word *Amen*, i.e., one word alone, is considered a contradiction to this directive. See *Berachos* 43a, *Rambam, Mishneh Torah, Hilchos Berachos* 7:6, and other sources.

which he wished to convey, takes up less words than the directive "One should not speak during a meal...." Seemingly, it would have been more appropriate to make that statement alone.

It has been suggested[9] that with the statement: "One should not speak during a meal...," Rav Yitzchak was not explaining why he would not share a Torah concept with Rav Nachman.[10] Instead, he was reproving Rav Nachman for speaking with him in the midst of a meal.[11] Since special priority is given to statements which are intended to dissociate a person from a transgression[12] over other words of Torah,[13] Rav Yitzchak made this brief statement. {He did not, by contrast, tell him: "Yaakov Avinu did not die...," for that statement has no relevance with regard to one's immediate conduct.[14] Therefore, there is no need for it to be made in the midst of a meal.}

9. The commentary of *Rif* (Reb Yoshiyahu Pinto) to *Ein Yaakov*.
10. *Rashi* offers such an explanation, that Rav Yitzchak was explaining his conduct.
11. This interpretation is reinforced by the version of the text quoted by the *Dikdukei Sofrim* which states: "Share a word of *aggadita* (homiletic teachings)." See also note 14.
12. For this reason, several prohibitions are waived for this purpose: e.g., the prohibition against giving *halachic* directives in the presence of one's teacher (see *Eruvin* 63a; *Rambam, Mishneh Torah, Hilchos Talmud Torah* 5:3), and the prohibition against speaking words of Torah in a bath house (*Shabbos* 40b; *Rambam, Mishneh Torah, Hilchos Krias Shema* 3:5).
13. See the notes of the *Pri Megadim (Eshel Avraham* 1*)* to *Orach Chayim* 170 which quotes this *Talmudic* passage and concludes: "It thus appears that to dissociate a person from transgression, one may speak. [This is allowed,] despite the principle: Danger to life is considered more severe than transgression."
14. See the gloss of *Iyun Yaakov* to the *Ein Yaakov*. Note, however, that there is a practical point which emerges from this concept with regard to the laws of ritual impurity. For a corpse conveys ritual impurity, and a living being does not. See *Niddah* 70b. This relates to the well-known discussion of whether the graves of *tzaddikim* convey ritual

This interpretation, however, also appears insufficient. Were this his intent, seemingly it would have sufficed for him to have said: "One should not speak during a meal," and not to have continued speaking in the midst of the meal. The rationale for this law, "lest the windpipe open before the esophagus, causing danger" is unnecessary.

True, adding this rationale does impress a listener with the severity of the matter, because "danger to life is considered more severe than transgression."[15] Nevertheless, for that very reason, seemingly, in the midst of a meal, one should confine oneself to a brief directive, for that is sufficient to dissociate the person from the transgression. After the conclusion of the meal, the rationale for the prohibition could have been added.

b) The manner in which concepts are stated in the Torah is precise. Therefore, Rav Yitzchak's statement that "Yaakov Avinu did not die" which he made after the meal appears to be connected with the statement he made during the meal, that "One should not speak during a meal...."[16] [How are they related?]

c) Rav Nachman's reply: "Was it for naught that he was mourned, embalmed, and buried?" is problematic. Seemingly, he should have said: Since Yaakov did not die, why was he mourned, embalmed, and buried?[17]

d) What is the significance of his reply, quoting the verse: "Do not fear, My servant Yaakov." Seemingly, this

---

impurity or not. This is not the place for extended discussion about this matter.

15. *Chulin* 10a. *Tur* and *Shulchan Aruch (Orach Chayim* 173:2).

16. See an explanation of this concept from a mystical perspective at the beginning of the text *Toras Levi Yitzchak.*

17. See the comments of the *Iyun Yaakov.* Note also the quote in *Eitz Yosef* to *Ein Yaakov.*

does not answer the question: "Was it for naught that he was mourned, embalmed, and buried?"[18]

There are commentaries[19] who explain that by identifying his source as the verse: "Do not fear," and extrapolating "Just as his descendants are alive, he is alive," Rav Yitzchak was explaining his original intent. His statement that Yaakov did not die was not meant to be taken in an absolutely literal sense, that his physical body did not die. For indeed, in this context, he did die. Instead, he was speaking about "the life of the soul."

This explanation, however, is difficult to accept. (If this is the intent, what is the new concept conveyed by the statement: "Yaakov Avinu did not die"? The "life of the soul" of all *tzaddikim* is eternal. Moreover,) it does not concur with *Rashi's* interpretation of the passage. *Rashi* states that Yaakov was embalmed, because "they thought that he had died." And afterwards,[20] he writes: "It appeared to them that he had died, but he was alive." From this, it is apparent[21] that *Rashi* interprets the statement: "Yaakov Avinu did not die" in the most literal sense, that his body did not die, as he writes: "he did not die, rather, he lives forever."

e) According to *Rashi's* commentary, the explanation does not appear to be contained in the text.[22] The answer to the question "Was it for naught that they mourned?..." is that it only *appeared* to them that he had died. (And this

---

18. See the gloss of *Rif* to *Ein Yaakov*, and the gloss of the *Anaf Yosef*.
19. *Chiddushei Aggados* of the *Maharsha* to *Taanis*, *loc. cit; Rashba, Ein Yaakov.*
20. Entry *af hu bachayim.*
21. This perspective also appears to be shared by *Tosafos* as mentioned previously (note 4), and by *Rashi's* commentary to the Torah. See *Likkutei Sichos*, Vol. IV, p. 1260ff. and Vol. XXVI, p. 7ff.
22. See the *Chiddushei Aggados* of the *Maharsha, loc. cit.*

is not stated in the *Talmud*.) The extrapolation from the verse merely brings proof that Yaakov did not die. It does not resolve the difficulty raised by Rav Nachman.

II. It is possible to resolve the above difficulties by seeing this passage in the context of its place in the *Talmud*. This story follows several other dialogues between Rav Nachman and Rav Yitzchak in which Rav Yitzchak replies: "Rabbi Yochanan said the following:..." The statements which he quotes in the name of Rabbi Yochanan all explain the miraculous nature of G-d's conduct with regard to the Jewish people.

For example, the first of the passages mentioned there states:[23]

> [With regard to the verse,[24] "In the first month, He has granted you the first rain, and the final rain."] Rav Nachman said to Rav Yitzchak: "Do the first rains descend in Nissan? The first rains descend in MarCheshvan...."

> [Rav Yitzchak] told him: "[The promise of] this verse was fulfilled in the days of Yoel ben Pasuel, as it is written.... That year, Adar passed without having any rain descend. The first rains descended on the first day of Nissan. The prophet told the Jewish people: "Go out and sow [your fields]."

> They answered him: "If a person has a measure of wheat, or a measure of barley, should he eat it and live, or should he sow it and die."

> He told them: "Notwithstanding [your logic], go out and sow."

23. *Taanis* 5a.
24. [*Yoel* 2:23.]

A miracle was wrought on their behalf and the kernels [concealed] in the walls and in the ant hives were revealed for them. [They sowed] them on the second, third, and fourth days. On the fifth day of Nissan, the second rain descended. And on the sixteenth of Nissan, they offered the *omer* Thus grain [which usually] grows in sixth months, grew in eleven days.

Following the statements from Rabbi Yochanan of this nature, the *Talmud* relates the story of Rav Yitzchak and Rav Nachman dining together. We can assume that when Rav Nachman asked Rav Yitzchak to share a Torah thought, Rav Nachman also knew that, because of the possible danger, one should not speak during a meal. Nevertheless, he thought that this prohibition applied only to ordinary talk,[25] and not to the words of the Torah.

When speaking words of the Torah, one might think that there is no need to worry about danger, because "the Torah protects and saves."[26] Indeed, we are obligated to recite words of Torah at a meal as reflected by the *Mishnah*:[27] "When three eat at one table without speaking words of Torah there, it is as if they ate of sacrifices to the dead..." Thus there is no need to worry about danger. When the Jews are occupied in Torah study (as commanded by G-d), G-d will protect them even in situations when, according to the natural order, there is a possibility of danger.

For this reason, Rav Yitzchak gave a full reply to Rav Nachman, mentioning not only the directive, "One should

25. See the gloss of the *Iyun Yaakov* to *Ein Yaakov* which explains a similar concept, albeit with a slightly different thrust.
26. *Sukkah* 21a.
27. *Avos* 3:3. See note 29.

not speak during a meal," but also the rationale, "lest the windpipe open before the esophagus, causing danger." With this rationale, he demonstrates that the prohibition applies[28] also to the words of Torah.[29]

To cite a parallel concept: It is written:[30] "One who observes a commandment will not know evil." And we have been taught: "Agents [charged with the performance of] a *mitzvah* will not be harmed."[31] Nevertheless, we can-

---

28. The *Iyun Yaakov* explains that it is permitted to speak words of Torah in the midst of a meal. The prohibition, however, applies to the ordinary talk of Sages which, [though ordinarily a worthy pursuit as reflected by our Sages' *(Sukkah 21b, Avodah Zorah 19b)* comment: "even the casual conversation of scholars demands study,"] is not permitted during a meal, because of the danger.

29. *Rabbeinu Chananel* concludes: "It is forbidden to speak words of *Halachah* in the midst of a meal."

   The *Magen Avraham (Orach Chayim* 170:1) states: "It is forbidden to speak even words of Torah during a meal." Afterwards, however, he states: "Whenever words of Torah are not spoken at a table, it is as if those who ate partook of sacrifices to the dead." It would appear that his intent is that words of Torah should be spoken either at the beginning of the meal or at the end, as explained in the *Aruch HaShulchan*.

   The *Perishah*, commenting on the *Tur (loc. cit.)*, states that it appears that it is forbidden to talk between one course and another course as long as one desires to continue eating. (Note the proof he quotes.) The *Eliyahu Rabbah*, however, differs and states that it is permitted to speak between courses. (His statements are quoted by the *Mishnah Berurah*.)

   In his gloss to *Ein Yaakov, Rif* states: "Since he desired to rebuke him, he stopped eating so that he could reply." This appears to imply that Rav Yitzchak ceased eating entirely, and did not resume; he was not merely pausing between courses. From the continuation of the passage [which states, "after he finished eating,"] however, it appears that this is not so.

   This is not the place for extended discussion about this matter.

30. *Koheles* 8:5. See the discussion of this concept in *Sdei Chemed,* Vol. III, p. 665b ff.; Vol. IX, p. 1880c ff.

31. *Pesachim* 8b.

not rely on this principle "in a situation where harm is probable,"[32] as reflected in the narrative to follow:[31]

> ([G-d commanded Shmuel the prophet] to anoint David. Although Shmuel was sent by G-d, he was frightened,)[33] as it is written:[34] "Shmuel said, 'How can I go? Shaul will hear, and he will kill me.'"

> "And G-d replied: 'Take a calf [to offer as a sacrifice].' [I.e., do not rely on the mitzvah to protect you, instead, employ a ruse.]"

To apply that concept in our context, since there is the possibility that "the windpipe open before the esophagus, causing danger,"[35] this is considered an instance where "harm is probable." Therefore, one cannot rely on the protective influence of the Torah and its mitzvos and hence, even words of Torah should not be spoken during a meal.

III. Based on the above, it is possible to explain the continuation of the narrative: "After he finished eating, he told him: 'Rabbi Yochanan said the following: Yaakov Avinu did not die.'" According to the interpretation mentioned above, Rabbi Yochanan's statement: "One should not speak during a meal..." reflects a general concept that applies with regard to the effect of the Torah and its mitzvos on the world at large. As Rabbi Yochanan emphasizes, although there are times when G-d works miracles for the

---

32. Pesachim, loc. cit. Rabbeinu Chananel has a slightly different version of the text which reads "where danger is set." This version is also found in Yoma 11a, Kiddushin 32b, and Chulin 142a.
33. Rashi, loc. cit.
34. I Shmuel 16:2.
35. The Talmud's expression which literally means "and he will come to danger," is quoted by the Rambam, as cited in footnote 8 and by the Shulchan Aruch HaRav.

Jewish people which transcend the natural order, by and large, a person's endeavors in the sphere of the Torah and its *mitzvos* must be enclothed within the natural order of the world. As such, although the Torah does bring about protection and deliverance, one cannot rely on this in a situation where harm is probable and miracles are required.

This concept — that our endeavors in the observance of the Torah and its *mitzvos* must be enclothed within the natural order of the world — can be explained in two ways: Either that the natural order requires such conduct, or that the Torah requires it.

a) This is required by the natural order. Since the laws of nature are a creation of G-d, G-d does not desire that the Torah and its *mitzvos* be observed in a manner that nullifies the natural order. As *Rabbeinu Nissim* writes:[36] "It is G-d's desire and will to maintain the natural order to the greatest degree possible. The natural order is precious in His eyes, and He does not negate it unless it is absolutely necessary to do so."[37]

b) This is required by the Torah, i.e., the purpose of the Torah and its *mitzvos* is to affect the natural order of the world, and not to modify it.

According to the first explanation, our endeavors within the Torah and its *mitzvos* must be enclothed within the natural order, because (since the Torah and its *mitzvos* were given within our world), they are governed by the rules of nature, (as it were). Therefore, the observance of the Torah is limited to situations where that observance is possible according to the rules of nature.

---

36. *Derashos HaRan*, Discourse 8, Introduction 1.
37. See also *Sefer HaChinuch, mitzvah* 546.

The second interpretation, by contrast, does not view the natural order as being able to confine or limit a person's observance of the Torah and its *mitzvos*. [The limitation is willful.] For the Torah prescribes that our observance must be enclothed within the world,[38] (rather than negate the natural order of the world).

IV. It is possible to say that these two approaches lie at the crux of the difference of opinion between Rav Yitzchak and Rav Nachman.

When, after eating, Rav Yitzchak quoted Rabbi Yochanan's statement: "Yaakov Avinu did not die," his intent was to [highlight the second of the opinions mentioned above]. The fact that the observance of the Torah and its *mitzvos* must be enclothed within the natural order is not because the laws of nature can control the Torah and its *mitzvos*.

On the contrary, as indicated by the statement: "Yaakov Avinu did not die," not only are the Torah and its *mitzvos* not confined by the limits of nature, they transcend that sphere entirely.

According to the laws of nature, death is an unequivocal reality, for it is impossible for a limited created being, subject to change, to exist with eternal vitality.[39] Nevertheless, Yaakov Avinu did not die. Yaakov was "the chosen of the Patriarchs,"[40] and as such, his entire existence was

---

38. See *Likkutei Sichos,* Vol. V, p. 80ff.

39. See *Emunos VeDeos* of Rav Saadia Gaon, Discourse 1, ch. 1; *Moreh Nevuchim,* Vol. II, Introduction 12; *Likkutei Sichos, op. cit.,* p. 97ff., and sources cited there.

40. As reflected by the verse *(Tehillim* 135:4): "Yaakov was chosen by G-d for Himself" *(Bereishis Rabbah* 76:1). See also *Zohar,* Vol. I, p. 171a; also p. 147b, 119b. See also *Shaar HaPesukim LehaAriZal, Toldos,* 27:24.

the Torah,[41] as it is written:[42] "Yaakov was a simple man, a dweller of tents." Therefore, just as the natural order does not limit the Torah itself, it cannot restrict Yaakov.[43]

Rav Nachman, by contrast, follows the first approach mentioned above. He interpreted Rabbi Yochanan's teaching forbidding speaking in the midst of a meal because of the danger that might arise as indicating that the Torah is limited by the natural order.

This is the intent of his reply: "Was it for naught that he was mourned, embalmed, and buried?" (He did not ask, if Yaakov was alive, why were these deeds performed? Instead,) his intent was that the fact that the Torah relates how Yaakov was mourned, embalmed, and buried, and tells that these activities were performed at the instruction of Yosef[44] (— indeed, the burial, which is a *mitzvah,* was performed based on the instructions of both Yaakov and Yosef —) indicates that the Torah recognizes the limitations of the natural order. If one were to say that "Yaakov did not die," the Torah's description of the activities performed with Yaakov's body is not true according to the Torah. (According to this conception, these activities would have been performed "for naught," only because of

---

41. See the gloss of the *Rashba* to *Ein Yaakov.* Note also the sources mentioned in note 43.

42. *Bereishis* 25:27. [The commentaries explain that "tents" refer to "the tents of the Torah."]

43. Similarly, with regard to Moshe, it is said *(Sotah* 13b; *Zohar,* Vol. 1, p. 37b):* "Moshe did not die." For Moshe is also identified with the Torah.

    The connection between Moshe and Yaakov is reflected by the *Tikkunei Zohar (Tikkun* 13, p. 29a) which states: "Moshe reflects the inner dimension, and Yaakov, the external dimension." See *Likkutei Sichos,* Vol. XXVI, p. 6ff.

44. *Bereishis* 50:2. See the commentary of the *Alshich* (quoted in the *Eitz Yosef)* which states that Yaakov's body remained intact when he was embalmed. See also the Responsa of the *Chasam Sofer, Yoreh De'ah,* Responsum 336.

this mistaken perception of the Egyptians who did not know that he did not die.)

In response to this objection, Rav Yitzchak states: "My statements are based on a *verse*.... Just as his descendants are alive, he too is alive." When he said, "Yaakov Avinu did not die," Rabbi Yochanan was not referring to the dimension of Yaakov's being that could be appreciated by the Egyptians, but rather, his *true being* (which applies also to his bodily existence).

Yaakov's true being is as it is conceived by the Torah, and this is not bound by the limitations of nature. Instead, "he is alive." This is implied by Rav Yitzchak's words: "My statements are based on a verse.... Just as his descendants are alive, he too is alive." Although from a material perspective (i.e., as the Egyptians view existence), this could not be perceived, as the concept exists in the Torah, and is extrapolated, [Yaakov's true life can be appreciated].

As such, there is no contradiction between the concept that Yaakov did not die, and the fact that "he was mourned...." He was mourned, embalmed, and buried, because as the Egyptians perceived reality, it appeared to them that he had died. For from their perspective, this concept was true (according to the Torah).[45] Hence they performed these activities with Yaakov's body. For the expression of the Torah and its *mitzvos* as they are enclothed in the matters of the world is a true expression of the Torah's intent.

---

45. Perhaps this is *Rashi's* intent in his choice of the words: "It appeared to them that he had died," as opposed to his previous statement: "They thought that he had died." Since "it appeared to them that he had died," they were required to act according to their perception.

Nevertheless, the apparent redundancy in *Rashi's* statements still requires an explanation. This, however, is not the place for it.

And thus, both aspects are true according to the Torah:
As they exist independently *(far zich)*, the Jews and the
Torah are not bound by the natural limitations of the
world. Nevertheless, G-d desired that the effects of the
observance of the Torah and its *mitzvos* be enclothed
within the natural order of the world. [And from that perspective, these activities are in place.]

V. Just as this above applies with regard to Yaakov
Avinu, "our grandfather Israel,"[46] so too, it applies with
regard to his descendants. "His descendants are alive."
This applies even as they exist in Egypt, "the nakedness of
the land,"[47] and in all the subsequent exiles, for "all the
ruling nations are described with the term *Mitzrayim,
Egypt.*"[48] The Jews are "the smallest among the nations,"[49]
and "one lamb among seventy wolves,"[50] and thus they
are "in a situation where harm is probable," physical
harm, and even more so, spiritual harm. Nevertheless,
concerning them it is said: "'Do not fear, My servant
Yaakov,' speaks G-d, 'And do not dismay, O Israel. For I
will deliver you from afar, and your descendants from the
land of their captivity.'" An association is established
between [Yaakov] and his descendants. Just as his
descendants are alive...." Even as Yaakov's descendants
exist in captivity and exile, they remain alive. For "you
who cling to G-d, your L-rd, are all alive."[51] Although the
natural laws of probability would not allow for this, these
natural laws do not determine the Jews' future.

---

46. *Rashi's* wording in *Taanis, loc. cit.*
47. *[Cf. Bereishis* 42:12.]
48. See *Bereishis Rabbah* 16:4.
49. *Devarim* 7:6.
50. See *Midrash Tanchuma, Parshas Toldos,* sec. 5; *Esther Rabbah* 10:11.
51. *Devarim* 4:5.

Thus we see two dimensions of the Torah and the Jewish people: a) as they "sit at a repast," i.e., as they are enclothed in the material dimensions of existence, in which instance, even their Torah activity recognizes the limits of the world. (Therefore, we do not speak words of the Torah in a place where harm is likely.)

b) as they exist "after eating," above the material plane, after they have completed the task of refining the material world. At that time, the essential quality of the Jews which transcends the natural order will be revealed, and it will be seen that "Yaakov did not die," and that "just as his descendants are alive, he too, is alive."

VI. Although we find the application of the concept of the eternality of physical existence with regard to Yaakov alone, when focusing on its inner dimensions, it can be applied to all Jews. As the *Mishnah* states:[52] "All Israel have a portion in the World to Come."

In this context, the term "World to Come" refers to the Era of Resurrection.[53] The rationale for this is reflected in the prooftext quoted by the *mishnah*:[54] "And your people are all righteous; they shall inherit the Land forever. [They are] the branch of My planting, the work of My hands in which to take pride."

Since they are "the branch of My planting, the work of My hands" — G-d's handiwork, as it were — all Israel will

---

52. *Sanhedrin* 10:1.
53. Rav Ovadiah of Bartenura and others.

    This is evident from the continuation of the *mishnah:* "The following do not have a portion in the World to Come: One who says the Resurrection of the Dead does not have a source in the Torah." As the *Talmud (Sanhedrin* 90a): states: "He denied the Resurrection; therefore, he will not have a share in this Resurrection.... Measure for measure."
54. *Yeshayahu* 60:21.

arise at the Resurrection of the Dead. Even their bodies
will exist with eternal vitality.[55]

This is transferred as an inheritance from Yaakov
Avinu, who did not die. In particular, this applies because
Yaakov was "the chosen of the Patriarchs,"[40] chosen by
G-d Himself. And with regard to G-d's choice of the Jewish
people, the *Tanya* explains[56] that G-d's choice of the Jewish people applies not only to their souls (which are "an
actual part of G-d from above"),[57] but also (and primarily)
to their bodies.

Thus the mourning and burying of Yaakov, which was
required by Torah because it *appeared* to them that he
died, draws down the potential for every Jew to reach the
Resurrection of the Dead through the task of refining and
purifying the body. This refinement is accomplished
through the negation of the body, via its return to dust[58]
(which as explained,[59] can be fulfilled through the spiritual
service of "My soul will be as dust to all,"[60] in which case
there is no need to actually return to dust). This brings us
to the Resurrection of the Dead in the true and ultimate
Redemption.

---

55. See the *maamar Lehavin Inyan Techiyas HaMeisim, Sefer HaMaamarim
Melukat,* Vol. III, p. 33ff [English Trans.: *Anticipating the Redemption*
(SIE, N.Y., 1994)].

56. Ch. 49 (69b), which states that G-d's essential choice of the Jewish
people is reflected in their physical bodies. See also *Toras Shalom,* p.
120.

57. *Tanya,* ch. 2.

58. Cf. *Bereishis* 3:19.

59. *Sefer HaSichos 5748,* Vol. I, (pp. 227-228); *Sefer HaMaamarim Melukat,*
Vol. II, p. 280.

60. *Berachos* 17a, the passage *Elokai netzor* recited after *Shemoneh Esreh.*

A Perplexing
Purim Feast

Adapted from *Likkutei Sichos*, Vol. XXXI, p. 177ff.

UNDERSTANDING OUR SAGES' CONDUCT	Our Sages state:[1] "A person is obligated to become intoxicated on Purim to the extent that he does not know the difference

between 'Cursed is Haman' and 'Blessed is Mordechai.'"
To cite an example, the *Talmud* continues, relating:

> Rabbah and Rav Zeira celebrated the Purim feast together. They became intoxicated. Rabbah stood up and slew Rav Zeira. On the morrow, he prayed for mercy and brought him back to life.

> The following year, [Rabbah] again invited [Rav Zeira] to celebrate the feast together. Rav Zeira answered him: "A miracle does not happen every moment."

---

1   *Megillah* 7b.

The story begs explanation.[2] How is it possible that one of the *Talmud's* leading Sages performed an act that — were it not for a miracle — would have resulted in a colleague's death?[3]

The *Maharsha*[4] indeed tries to explain that Rabbah did not actually slay Rav Zeira. Instead, he compelled him to drink extensively until he became sick and was at the brink of death. This interpretation, however, does not fit the simple meaning of the text which speaks of Rav Zeira being slain and then "brought back to life." Moreover, even such conduct, compelling a person to drink to the point that his life is in danger, is not appropriate for a Torah sage.

There is another element of the story which is also problematic: Rabbah's invitation to Rav Zeira to repeat the feast the following year. The *Talmud* does not tell us that Rabbah repented; quite the contrary, it explains that he was prepared to share a Purim feast with Rav Zeira again despite the possibility of a recurrence of the events of the previous year.

---

2.   The *Chasam Sofer (Orach Chayim,* Responsa 185, 196*)* connects this story with our Sages' statement *(Shabbos 156a)* that a person born under the sign of Mars will shed blood, for Rabbah himself said: "I was born under the sign of Mars."

      Nevertheless, as the *Rambam* emphasizes *(Shemoneh Perakim,* ch. 8; *Mishneh Torah, Hilchos Teshuvah 5:4),* a person is not controlled by his natural tendencies. Moreover, these tendencies themselves can be used for a positive purpose, as our Sages *(Shabbos, op. cit.)* continue, explaining that a person born under the sign of Mars can become a doctor, a *mohel,* or a ritual slaughterer.

3.   Although Rabbah was intoxicated, our Sages rule *(Bava Kamma 26a; Rambam, Mishneh Torah, Hilchos Choveil U'Mazik* 1:11*):* "A person is always responsible for his actions, whether [performed] consciously or unconsciously, whether he is awake, asleep, or drunk."

4.   *Chiddushei Aggados,* commenting on *Megillah, loc. cit.* See also the *Hagahos Ya'abetz* which offers a similar interpretation.

And what is equally amazing is Rav Zeira's answer. He did not refuse Rabbah's invitation categorically. Instead, he told him: "A miracle does not happen every moment," implying that he would like to accept Rabbah's offer, but could not because he was not sure that the miracle would repeat itself.

NOT MERELY ALLEGORY There are those[5] who explain the story as reflecting spiritual concepts. But it would be wrong to say that it is a mere allegory,[6] for:

a) the story is quoted as an example of the fulfillment of the directive: "A person is obligated to become intoxicated on Purim...." Just as the law must be fulfilled in actual deed, so, too, the example must have actually occurred.

b) Rabbeinu Efraim[7] uses the example of Rabbah's conduct to argue that the *Talmud* did not accept the law that "A person is obligated to become intoxicated on Purim...."

From either perspective, it is clear that the story of Rabbah and Rav Zeira is not merely a spiritual allegory, but a chronicle of an event that actually took place.

Thus an explanation must be found which:

a) interprets the story according to its simple meaning — that the two Sages actually became intoxicated and Rabbah caused Rav Zeira's death — and yet;

---

5. For example, the *maamar* entitled *Omar Rava*, 5708; *Likkutei Levi Yitzchak al Maamarei Chazal*, p. 178; *Tzafnas Paneach al HaTorah*, Parshas Vayechi 49:22.

6. As some interpret the stories associated with Rabbah bar bar Chanah in *Bava Basra* 73b.

7. Quoted by Rabbeinu Nissim and the *Baal HaMeor* in their *halachic* commentaries to *Megillah, loc. cit.*

b) projects an image of the Sages that is befitting their spiritual stature, one which explains how Rabbah's actions can in no way be associated with murder and why Rav Zeira would have desired to repeat the feast the following year.

"WHEN WINE ENTERS, THE SECRETS COME OUT" A resolution can be reached through comparison to another tragedy associated with excessive drinking: the death of Aharon's sons, Nadav and Avihu. For as our Sages state,[8] they died because they entered the Sanctuary while intoxicated.

In this context, a question is raised: Aharon's sons were on a high spiritual level. Indeed, Moshe himself said that their rung of refinement surpassed his own and that of Aharon.[9] How then was it possible for them to conduct themselves in such an undesirable manner?

These questions can be resolved based on the commentary of the *Or HaChayim*, who explains the death of Nadav and Avihu as follows:[10]

> They came close to a sublime light with holy love, and died because of it. This is the mystic secret of "[G-d's] kiss" through which the righteous die. Their death was equivalent to the death of the righteous.

---

8.   *Vayikra Rabbah* 12:1, cited by *Rashi* in his commentary to *Vayikra* 10:2.

9.   As *Vayikra* 10:3 relates, Moshe told Aharon: "This is [the meaning of] what G-d said: 'I will be sanctified by those close to Me and I will be glorified before the entire nation.'" *Rashi* explains that Moshe was saying: "I knew that the Sanctuary would be consecrated by those in communion with G-d. I surmised that this would be either me or you. Now I see that they are greater than we are."

10. One of the interpretations he offers to *Leviticus* 16:1.

This indeed is alluded to by the Torah itself, which relates that "in drawing close to G-d, they died," implying that their death came as a result of their drawing close to G-d.[11]

On this basis, we can understand our Sages' statement that they entered the Sanctuary intoxicated. Wine is used as an analogy for the Torah's mystic secrets, as alluded to in our Sages' expression:[12] "When wine enters, the secrets come out." "Intoxicated with wine" implies that the appreciation of these mystic secrets overwhelmed their powers of thought, and led them to an inextinguishable yearning for G-d, resulting in the expiration of their souls.

This allegorical interpretation is not, however, divorced from actual fact. In addition to partaking of the Torah's mystic secrets, Aharon's sons also drank actual wine.[13] For since they were holy, the release of inhibitions which alcohol causes spurred their spiritual potentials. We find a parallel to this in a testimony of the Shaloh[14] who speaks of exceedingly holy people:

> Drink[ing] much more than ordinary at large feasts... with an intent for the sake of Heaven... They were in very good spirits and therefore, recited many Torah teachings.... For due to a spirit of happiness, a wise man will reveal the Torah's

---

11. See the maamar entitled Acharei, 5649; Likkutei Sichos, Vols. III and XXXII, Parshas Acharei, where these concepts are discussed. See also the essay entitled Souls Afire (In the Garden of the Torah, Vol. II) which discusses these concepts in English.
12. Eruvin 65a.
13. Entering the Sanctuary after doing so did not represent a sin, for the prohibition against entering the Sanctuary was not communicated until afterwards.
14. Shaar HaOsios, p. 84b.

mystic secrets.... as implied by the expression, "When wine enters, the secrets come out."[15]

THE DANGERS OF OVER-EXPOSURE On this basis, we can understand the intoxication that occurred at Rabbah and Rav Zeira's Purim feast. Rabbah and Rav Zeira partook freely of the "wine of Torah," i.e., they delved deeply into the Torah's mystic secrets. Rav Zeira died, i.e., his soul expired in yearning for G-dliness like the souls of Aharon's sons.

Why does the *Talmud* say that Rabbah "slew Rav Zeira"? The precise word the *Talmud* uses for slay is *vishachat.* Generally, when the *Talmud* describes a killing, it uses the word *ketal. Shachat* is the term used to refer to ritual slaughter. In the latter context, our Sages said:[16] "The sole meaning of *vishachat* ("and he slaughtered") is *umashach* "and he drew after."[17]

The name "Rabbah" means "the great one," i.e., he had a broad intellectual capacity. The name "Zeira," by contrast, means "the small one," i.e., he had a more lim-

---

15. To counter this tendency, the Torah commanded *(Vayikra* 10:9): "Do not drink wine or strong drink," which is interpreted (by *Rashi*) to mean: "Do not drink wine to the extent of intoxication."

A person's connection with the secrets of the Torah must be in moderation, so that he will not be in danger of his soul expiring with love for G-d. This is implied by the interpretation (see the sources mentioned in note 11) of our Sages' description *(Chagigah* 14b) of Rabbi Akiva's entry into the mystic experience described as the *Pardes:* "He entered in peace and he departed in peace," i.e., his entry was also "in peace," controlled and measured, so that he would "depart in peace."

16. *Chullin* 30b.

17. [With regard to ritual slaughter, the intent is that the slaughterer must draw the knife back and forth across the animal's neck until he cuts the windpipe and the esophagus. The term is being used according to its figurative meaning as explained above.]

ited capacity. During their feast, while Rabbah and Rav Zeira were indulging in deep mystic secrets — and drinking wine, in a manner parallel to that described by the *Shaloh* — Rabbah "stood up," i.e., he rose to a higher level of mystic understanding. *Vishachat liRav Zeira,* "he slew Rav Zeira," i.e., he drew Rav Zeira after him, sharing his knowledge with him. But because Rav Zeira did not have as great an intellectual capacity as Rabbah, he was unable to control himself, and his soul expired.

Rabbah's responsibility for Rav Zeira's death is thus merely an error of judgment; he thought that Rav Zeira could, as Rabbah himself did, contain his soul despite becoming aware of these mystical truths. Moreover, since Rabbah had the power to bring Rav Zeira back to life, the experience of *klos hanefesh,* that Rav Zeira's soul expired in love for G-d, was not a negative one. Ultimately, Rav Zeira was also able to "depart in peace,"[18] and return to a measured and controlled path of Divine service within this world.

FORCED TO DECLINE AN INVITATION On this basis, we can understand Rav Zeira's response to Rabbah's invitation the following year. Both Sages desired to repeat the experience. Rabbah hoped that in the year that had passed, Rav Zeira had progressed in his Divine service to the point that he would be able to receive the mystic secrets from Rabbah without having his soul expire. Rav Zeira also desired to taste these spiritual heights.

And yet, he had to decline the invitation. For he realized that the ultimate intent is to serve G-d within the context of our material existence. He was not sure that he

---

18. See note 15.

would be able to contain his soul in the face of the powerful revelations and feared that it would expire again. And since "A miracle does not happen every moment," he was not willing to take the risk that he would not be able to continue his life on the material plane.

KNOWING — AND NOT KNOWING   As mentioned above, the story of Rabbah and Rav Zeira is quoted as a support for the law that "A person is obligated to become intoxicated on Purim to the extent that he does not know the difference between 'Cursed is Haman' and 'Blessed is Mordechai.'"

The fact that this law is accepted by the *Shulchan Aruch*[19] indicates that we do not fear negative consequences, that Purim is a time when every person can rise to unbounded levels of love for G-d, and yet, return to controlled and measured Divine service on the material plane. For the heightened experience of this one day will impart energy and vitality to one's Divine service for the entire year.

---

19. *Orach Chayim* 695:2.

IS TRUE HUMILITY
POSSIBLE?

Adapted from *Likkutei Sichos*, Vol. XIII, p. 30ff.

A DOWNWARD SPIRAL The concluding *mishnah* of the tractate of *Sotah* emphasizes the pattern of spiritual descent that accompanied the destruction of the Second *Beis HaMikdash*. It mentions several Sages and underscores how they served as paradigms for various spiritual qualities, but relates that when those Sages died, these spiritual qualities — at least as expressed in a complete sense — were no longer manifest. The *mishnah* concludes stating, "When Rebbi (Rabbi Yehudah *HaNasi*) died, humility and the fear of sin were nullified."

The *Gemora* discusses the different points of the *mishnah* and concludes:

> Rav Yosef told the Sage relating the *mishnah,* "[When speaking of Rebbi,] do not say [that] humility [was nullified], for I exist." ("And I am humble," *Rashi*.) Rav Nachman told the Sage relating the *mishnah,* "[When speaking of Rebbi,] do

not say [that] the fear of sin [was nullified], for I exist."

POINTS TO PONDER   This narrative raises several conceptual difficulties. First and foremost, on the surface, Rav Yosef's statement: "Do not say [that] humility [was nullified], for I exist," hardly appears to epitomize humility.

Also, Rav Yosef and Rav Nachman were contemporaries and were aware of each other's greatness.[1] Why didn't they tell the sage reading the *mishnah* to eliminate the entire clause, taking into consideration, not only their own personal virtues, but also the positive qualities that the other possessed?

And we find that Rabbi Pinchas ben Yair states:[2] "Humility leads to the fear of sin." How could Rav Nachman see himself as a paradigm of the higher quality — fear of sin — and yet consider the necessary prerequisite for the attainment of that quality, humility, as "nullified"?[3]

---

1.   See *Kiddushin* 20b which records Rav Yosef's praise of Rav Nachman, and *Eruvin* 30a which records Rav Nachman's praise of Rav Yosef.

2.   *Avodah Zarah* 20b. In certain versions of the *Talmud,* this quote also appears as part of the *mishnah* — or as a *bereisa* — in the conclusion of *Sotah.*

3.   One might attempt to resolve this question by explaining that Rav Nachman follows the opinion of Rabbi Yehoshua ben Levi *(Avodah Zarah, loc. cit.;* see also *Jerusalem Talmud, Shekalim* 3:6) that humility is a greater virtue than the fear of sin. Thus Rav Nachman maintains that although he epitomized fear of sin, the quality of humility could in fact be nullified, for it is a higher virtue which he himself has not attained. Conversely, Rav Yosef does not mention that the fear of sin has not been nullified (although he sees himself as a paradigm of humility), because he follows the opinion of Rabbi Pinchas ben Yair which maintains that the fear of sin surpasses humility.

It is, however, difficult to offer this explanation, because there is no source which states that Rav Yosef and Rav Nachman perpetuated the

SELF-ASSURED HUMILITY To focus on the first of the difficulties which was raised: The definition of humility is not, as is popularly conceived, a sense of meekness and low self-image in which a person has no sense of his own worth.[4] Instead, a true sense of humility is complemented by self-assurance. The person radiates confidence and self-esteem, but has no trace of arrogance or boastful pride. He knows his personal virtues, exercises them productively, and yet this does not lead to egotism or haughtiness.

We see this fusion exemplified by Moshe, our teacher. He himself told the Jewish people:[5] "It is I who stands between G-d and you," and it was he who wrote the verse:[6] "And there never arose in Israel a prophet like Moshe." Nevertheless, he was "more humble than all the men on the face of the earth."[7]

Moshe did not see pride and humility as conflicting tendencies.[8] Although he knew the greatness of the mission he had been given, and realized that he had been granted unique personal traits to enable him to fulfill this mission, this knowledge did not lead to ego-conscious pride. On the contrary, he realized that he had been

---

difference of opinion between Rabbi Pinchas ben Yair and Rabbi Yehoshua ben Levi.

4. *Biurei Zohar, L'Admur HaEmtzaei, Parshas Pekudei*, p. 59b; *Tzemach Tzedek* p. 309. See also the essay entitled "Pride That Runs Deeper Than Self" in *In the Garden of the Torah*, Vol. II, p. 19ff.

5. *Devarim* 5:5.

6. *Devarim* 34:10.

7. *Bamidbar* 12:3.

8. There is a further corollary to this principle. Precisely because of his humility, Moshe was able to make full use of the potentials he had been granted. When a person is possessed by egocentric pride, much of his energy goes into feeding his ego rather than productive work. And moreover, his self-consciousness causes friction with others.

endowed with these potentials by G-d; they were not the fruit of his own efforts. Moreover, he believed that if these gifts had been given to another, that person might have achieved even more than he.[9]

For this reason, Moshe humbled himself before all those who approached him.[10] Nevertheless, when it was necessary for him to exercise his authority, he did so with all the force and power required.

| A HUMBLE MAN'S SELF-IMAGE | Similar concepts can be explained with regard to Rav Yosef. He too was aware of his |

virtues, but saw them as trusts endowed to him by G-d and realized that perhaps another person could have administered these trusts more effectively. And just as his appreciation of his other virtues did not lead to pride, so too, he was able to remain humble despite his awareness of his own humility.

This conception is also reflected in the phrase which Rav Yosef chose to express his own self-image:[11] "Many harvests are reaped through the power of an ox." An ox has nothing to be proud of, for the harvests are not the product of his labor. They stem from the power of growth contained within the seeds and within the earth. The ox is merely an intermediary whose efforts enable this power of growth to be harnessed and put to use.

---

9.   *Sefer HaMaamarim 5697*, p. 298ff.
10. I.e., not only did he not feel himself above anyone else (because his powers were given him by G-d and not the products of his own work), he also humbled himself before others (because he felt that someone else could have used those powers better than he did).
11. *Sanhedrin* 42a.

Similar concepts are reflected in the term used to describe Rav Yosef:[12] "the master of wheat." The implication is that the advantage is that the wheat — allegorically referring to the breadth of Torah knowledge Rav Yosef possessed — is a valuable resource. Rav Yosef is praised merely for being a fit reservoir for this resource to be stored.[13]

| **DOES STUDY LEAD TO INNER CHANGE?** There is, however, still room for question: Through studying the Torah, a person protects himself from the influence of the evil inclination and thus shields himself from sin. The attainment of this status was seemingly Rav Yosef's own personal achievement and did not come automatically, as a result of the potentials he was granted from above. Therefore he had ample justification for pride.

It can, however, be explained that — in protecting a person from sin — the Torah does not necessarily change the person's nature. According to Rav Yosef, when a person studies the Torah, he may remain who he is, the Torah merely exerts a protective influence from above. Therefore a person should rightfully be humble even though his Torah studies cause him to be protected from sin. For the fact that he is protected from sin does not represent a personal achievement. Instead, it is still

---

12. *Horios* 14a.
13. The concept of the fusion of humility and self-assurance is also communicated by another term that *Horios, op. cit.,* uses to refer to Rav Yosef: "Sinai."

Sinai is "the lowest of all the mountains," a symbol of humility, and yet it *is* a mountain, exemplifying confidence and power. See the essay entitled "The Revelation at Mt. Sinai," which develops these concepts *[Timeless Patterns in Time,* Vol. II, p. 109ff. (Kehot, N.Y., 1994)].

considered as a result of the influence which he is granted from above.

On this basis, we can also understand why Rav Nachman considered the quality of humility to have been nullified, although he was aware of Rav Yosef and his virtues. Rav Nachman maintains that the study of the Torah changes the nature of the person, and it is because of this inner transformation that he is protected from sin. This inner transformation can be considered as the person's own achievement and a just reason for pride.[14]

WHY RAV	Using similar reasoning, we can appre-
NACHMAN	ciate why Rav Yosef did not acknowl-
FEARED SIN	edge Rav Nachman's fear of sin. The

Talmud relates[15] that an astrologer told Rav Nachman's mother that her son would become a thief. Frightened over the fate of her child, she had him cover his head at all times so that he would be possessed by the fear of Heaven, and she prayed that the evil inclination would not take control of him. Once, his headcovering fell, and his evil inclination overpowered him.

Accordingly, Rav Yosef maintained that fear of sin was not an integral part of Rav Nachman's being, but rather an incremental factor dependent on his head being covered and his mother's prayers. Hence just as Rav Yosef did not attach importance to the fact that he himself was protected from sin by his Torah study, he did not consider Rav Nachman's fear of sin sufficient to amend the *mishnah* to say that the fear of sin had not been nullified.

---

14. Although Rav Yosef was in fact humble, in Rav Nachman's opinion, that humility stemmed from a lack of appreciation of his own positive virtues. And as mentioned above, a true sense of humility involves knowing one's virtues and yet remaining humble.

15. *Shabbos* 156b.

Rav Nachman, by contrast, maintained that even though at the outset his fear of sin had been caused by external factors, afterwards, these qualities became internalized. Thus he justly felt that his own conduct was noteworthy enough for the *mishnah* to be amended so that it would not mention the fear of sin being nullified.

CAN EXTERNALS BECOME INTERNALS? We thus see that Rav Nachman maintains that even though at the outset certain qualities may be incremental to a person's nature, ultimately they can become internalized to the extent that they characterize his personality. Rav Yosef, by contrast, maintains that an external factor can never be more than that. Although it may affect a person's conduct and control his habits, it does not change his nature.

This difference in approach is reflected in a difference of opinion between these Sages with regard to a point of *halachah*.[16] It is forbidden to recite the *Shema* near urine unless one pours water into it. All authorities agree that if a utensil already contains urine, it is necessary to pour a *revi'is* of water into it to nullify the urine's presence. When, however, a utensil is empty, and water is poured into it, and then urine, there is a difference between [the opinions of] Rav Nachman and Rav Yosef. Rav Nachman maintains that if the water precedes the urine, then any amount of water — even less than a *revi'is* — is sufficient to nullify the influence of the urine. Rav Yosef, by contrast, maintains that it makes no difference whether the water precedes the urine or not, at least a *revi'is* of water is always necessary.

---

16. *Berachos* 25b.

What is the difference between the two opinions? Rav Nachman maintains that if the water is poured into the container first, it brings about a fundamental change. Although the water itself is an increment, the fact that it is poured into the container first makes a difference, and it affects the container's future status. Rav Yosef does not accept this principle and maintains that the standard quantity of water is required at all times.

To apply these concepts to the previous discussion: Rav Nachman maintains that external factors — e.g., wearing a headcovering or studying Torah — can make a fundamental change in a person's nature. Therefore, he describes himself as fearing sin, and does not think it appropriate to describe Rav Yosef as humble. Rav Yosef, by contrast, maintains that external factors will not bring about internal change. Therefore, he does not consider Rav Nachman as fearing sin, and considers it appropriate to describe his own self as humble.

AN ULTIMATE SENSE OF HUMILITY

There still remains a difficulty to be resolved: It was explained that Rav Nachman did not consider Rav Yosef to be humble, because Rav Yosef had a virtue that he had attained through his own efforts. For this reason, the concept that all his virtues came as trusts from above and another person could have administered them more effectively did not apply to him. If this argument is true, how could the *mishnah* ascribe humility to Rebbi and the Torah ascribe humility to Moshe: surely they — like Rav Yosef — possessed positive virtues which they attained through their own efforts?

This question can be resolved by citing two conceptions of humility offered by our Sages.[17] As mentioned
previously, Rabbi Pinchas ben Yair states: "Humility leads
to the fear of sin," implying that he considers the fear of
sin as a greater virtue. Rabbi Yehoshua ben Levi, by contrast, maintains that humility is a greater virtue than the
fear of sin.

It can be explained that the Sages are not disagreeing.
Instead, each one is referring to a different level of humility.[18] There is one level of humility that is a function of
logic. Based on a particular set of reasons, e.g., the reasons
mentioned above — that we have been endowed with our
potentials by G-d, and if these gifts had been given to
another person, he might have achieved even more, a
person appreciates that he should be humble. There is,
however, a deeper approach to humility, one that is not
dependent on logical conclusions, but which comes from
an inner sense of selflessness.

What is the source for this potential? The humility of
G-d Himself, as our Sages comment:[19] "In the place of the
greatness of the Holy One, blessed be He, there you find
His humility."

G-d's humility is not motivated by any reason, but
rather is a fundamental element of His being. "The righteous resemble their Creator,"[20] and thus humility of this
nature is mirrored in certain great *tzaddikim*, for example,

---

17. *Avodah Zarah* 20b.
18. The *Talmud* uses the expression *piligei*, implying that there is a difference of opinion between them. Nevertheless, it is possible to interpret
that term (as does the *Shaloh, Hakdamah*, p. 36a) as referring to a difference in emphasis, but not a disagreement in principle.
19. *Megillah* 31a; see the explanation in *Sefer HaMaamarim 5700*, p. 40.
20. *Rus Rabbah* 4:3; See sources cited in *Likkutei Sichos*, Vol. IV, p. 1136,
fn. 6.

Moshe our teacher,[21] and Rebbi. Rav Nachman maintained, however, that in the era of exile, such humility
was no longer possible.[22]

There is, however, a positive connection between the
descent into exile and humility. All the revelations of that
future era are dependent on our Divine service in the era
of exile.[23] Thus it is this descent and the Divine service of
the Jewish people, despite the challenges of exile, which
will lead to the fulfillment of the prophecy:[24] "The humble
shall increase their joy in G-d," with the coming of the
Redemption. May this take place in the immediate future.

---

21. It was explained above that Moshe's humility came because of a
    rational calculation. This is true, but the very fact that Moshe was able
    to accept such a calculation was because he possessed the true and
    essential quality of humility mentioned above.
22. Rav Yosef, however, was focusing on the lower level of humility,
    which is accessible even in the era of exile. Therefore, he maintained
    that the clause mentioning humility should be removed from the
    mishnah, for he personified — at least — this lower level of humility.
23. *Tanya,* ch. 37.
24. *Yeshayahu* 29:19.

TO WHOM SHOULD THE TORAH BE GIVEN?

Adapted from *Likkutei Sichos,* Vol. XVIII, p. 28ff.

A NEIGHBORLY CLAIM	With regard to the giving of the Torah, our Sages relate:[1]

When Moshe ascended to the heavens, the ministering angels asked the Holy One, blessed be He: "Master of the world, what is one born of a mother doing among us?"

He told them: "[He came] to receive the Torah."

They protested: "There is a hidden treasure... and You desire to give it to flesh and blood. 'What is man that You shall remember him?'[2] 'G-d, our Master,... who places Your glory in the heavens.'[3]"

The Holy One, blessed be He, told Moshe: "Provide them with an answer."

---

1. *Shabbos* 88b.
2. *Tehillim* 8:5.
3. *Ibid.*:2.

[Moshe] responded before Him: "The Torah which You are going to give me, what is written in it? 'I am G-d, your L-rd, who took you out of the land of Egypt.'"[4]

[Moshe] told [the angels]: "Did you descend to Egypt? Were you enslaved to Pharaoh? Why should the Torah be yours?"

And he continued telling them: "What else is written in it? 'You shall have no other gods.'[5] Do you live among idol-worshipping nations?"

[And so, Moshe challenged the angels with regard to all the other commandments:] "Do you work?... Are you involved in business?... Do you have a father or a mother?... Is there envy among you?... Do you have an evil inclination?...."

[The angels] immediately acknowledged [the correctness of the choice of] the Holy One, blessed be He.

The Rabbis[6] explain that the angels' claim was based on the principle of *bar meitzra.* If a person sells his field, a person who owns a neighboring field has the right to buy the field from the purchaser at the price the purchaser paid.[7] The angels were claiming that since the Torah was hidden in the heavens, and they are heavenly beings, it would have been appropriate for the Torah to have been given to them.[8]

4. *Shmos* 20:2.
5. *Ibid.:*3.
6. *Shtei Yaddos* beginning of *Parshas Terumah; Pnei David, Parshas Yisro.*
7. *Bava Metzia* 108a; *Rambam, Mishneh Torah, Hilchos Shecheinim* 12:5; *Tur* and *Shulchan Aruch (Choshen Mishpat* 175:6).
8. Even though the Torah states: "Speak to the children of Israel," "Say to the children of Israel," and the like, the angels still claimed it as their

| **Rabbinic** | Among the resolutions offered by the |
| **Refutation** | Rabbis in response to the angels' |

claims are:

a) The privilege of *bar meitzra* is given to a neighbor only with regard to landed property, and not with regard to movable property.[9] Since the Torah is not landed property, the angels do not deserve this privilege.

b) The privilege of *bar meitzra* is given to a neighbor only with regard to a sale, but not with regard to a present.[10] Since the Torah was given to the Jews as a present,[11] this privilege is not granted.

c) The privilege granted to a neighbor does not apply if the purchaser is a relative of the seller. Since the Jews are closely related to G-d, "You are children of G-d your L-rd,"[12] the protests of the angels are of no consequence.

d) Moshe is described as "the man of G-d."[13] The *Midrash* relates that "From his waist down, he was a man; from his waist up, he was G-dly." Thus Moshe was also a neighbor to the Torah, and he had as valid a claim to it as the angels did.

e) Our Sages comment:[14] "Whoever rules with truth and faithfulness in a judgment becomes a partner with the Holy One, blessed be He, in the work of creation." Moshe

---

own. For even after a sale has been completed and a bill of sale mentioning the purchaser drawn up, a neighbor has the right to claim the field for himself.

9. *Maggid Mishneh*, gloss to *Hilchos Shecheinim* 13:4, *Tur* and *Shulchan Aruch, loc. cit.*:53.

10. *Rambam, loc. cit.* 13:1, *Tur* and *Shulchan Aruch, loc. cit.*:54.

11. See *Berachos* 5a, *Bereishis Rabbah* 6:5, *et al.* Indeed, in our prayers we continually refer to G-d as "the *Giver* of the Torah," and speak of Shavuos as "the season of the *giving* of the Torah."

12. *Devarim* 14:1.

13. *Devarim* 33:1; *Tehillim* 90:1.

14. *Shabbos* 10a.

is cited as the epitome of a person delivering a true judgment.

When a person is a partner with a person who sells property, he has the right to purchase such property despite the protests of a neighbor.[15] Since Moshe delivered true judgments and became a partner with G-d, he had a right to the Torah despite the protests of the angels.[16]

AND THEIR REFUTATION   These proposed resolutions, however, are not entirely acceptable. Firstly, the last two explanations involve Moshe individually, and not the Jewish people. And it is to the Jewish people as a whole that the Torah was given.[17] But more fundamentally, none of these explanations appears to reflect the replies which Moshe gave to the angels. On the contrary, the last three proposed resolutions appear to run contrary to the thrust of Moshe's replies. For the resolutions emphasize the spiritual qualities of Moshe and/or the Jewish people, while Moshe's replies appear to underscore the fact that the Jews live in a material environment and must contend with negative influences.

---

15. *Rambam, loc. cit.* 12:5, *Tur* and *Shulchan Aruch, loc. cit.*:49.
16. This explanation follows the opinion that Yisro came to Moshe [and observed him judging the Jewish people] before the giving of the Torah *(Zevachim* 116a).
17. It is possible to explain that not only Moshe, but the entire Jewish people are "neighbors" of the Torah, because the source of their souls is "from below [G-d's] throne of glory" *(Zohar,* Vol. III, p. 29b). Moreover, the entire people (not only Moshe) can be considered as G-d's partners. For it is said *(Shabbos* 119b): "Whoever recites the passage *Vayichulu* on the *Shabbos* eve, becomes a partner with the Holy One, blessed be He, in the work of creation," and the Jews were commanded regarding the observance of the *Shabbos* before the giving of the Torah *(Sanhedrin* 56b). Nevertheless, as will be explained, it is the fundamental thrust of these proposed resolutions, not merely their particulars, which is problematic.

There is also another difficulty with the first proposed resolution — that the privilege of *bar meitzra* is granted to a neighbor only with regard to landed property and the Torah is not landed property. The reason this privilege is granted only with regard to landed property and not with regard to movable property is that it is to the neighbor's advantage to have two fields located next to each other instead of having to purchase another field in a further removed place. Such a difficulty would not arise with regard to movable property, for as its name implies, once it is purchased, it can be taken by the purchaser to his own place.

Thus this concept does not apply to the Torah, for the Torah cannot be obtained anywhere else but from G-d. And once it has been given, it no longer shares the same connection to the place — the spiritual realms — from which it originates, for as our Sages emphasize,[18] after the giving of the Torah, it is "no longer in the heavens."

Similarly, the second of the proposed resolutions, that the privilege given to a neighbor applies only with regard to a sale and the Torah was given as a present, is also problematic. For we also find the concept of a sale identified with G-d's granting the Jews the Torah.[19] Thus in allegorical terms, our Sages quote G-d as saying:[20] "I sold My Torah to you."

THERE IS ONLY ONE TORAH	There are other explanations offered with regard to the passage cited above. There are four ap-

---

18. *Bava Metzia* 59b.
19. In addition, we find (see the sources mentioned in note 10), that if the giver takes responsibility for the present he gives, the neighbor is granted the privilege of purchasing the field.
20. *Shmos Rabbah* 33:1; see also *Berachos* 5a which uses the analogy of a sale with regard to the giving of the Torah.

proaches to the Torah: *pshat,* the simple meaning, *remez,* the allusions, *derush,* the allegories, and *sod,* the mystic dimension. The *Alshich*[21] explains that the angels did not issue a claim with regard to the *pshat* of the Torah; they knew that belonged to the Jewish people. They laid claim to the *sod,* the Torah's mystic dimension. They felt that since these teachings are purely spiritual, they belong in the heavens, and should not be given to mortals but rather to the angels themselves, for they are "neighbors."

This claim, however, can also be refuted. The law[22] is that when a person sells all of his properties, a person whose land borders on only one of the properties cannot claim the privileges of a neighbor, for the sale must be viewed as an integral whole. Similarly, with regard to the angels' claim, the simple meaning of the Torah and its mystic dimension are both part of a single integral unit; they cannot be divided from each other.

This explanation, moreover, is also not reflected in Moshe's replies to the angels. On the contrary, his statements: "Did you descend to Egypt? Were you enslaved to Pharaoh?... Do you work?... Are you involved in business?..." were factors which this explanation had seemingly taken for granted.

NOT FOR PROFIT   Another proposed resolution is based on the following law:[23] If a person seeks to purchase a field because he is in a pressing financial situation and needs the field to earn his livelihood, while a neighbor seeks to purchase it merely

---

21. Commentary to *Tehillim*, psalm 8; see also *Chiddushei Aggados* of the *Maharsha* to *Shabbos* 88b, which offers a similar explanation.
22. *Bava Metzia* 108b; *Rambam, loc. cit.,* 12:6; *Tur* and *Shulchan Aruch, loc. cit.*:36.
23. *Ramah, Choshen Mishpat* 175:49.

for the sake of added income, the neighbor is not granted the privileges of a *bar meitzra*.

The Jews require the Torah for their very existence, as we say in our prayers,[24] it is "our life and the length of our days." And it is only through the Torah that we can overcome the evil inclination. Thus our Sages quoted G-d as saying,[25] "I created the evil inclination, and I created the Torah as a condiment for it."

Thus the Jews can be compared to a purchaser who is in a difficult situation and requires the property in question to maintain his existence. The angels, by contrast, appear to resemble the neighbor who is seeking merely additional profit. In such a situation, the angels' claim is not accepted.

This resolution does relate to the some of the replies Moshe gave the angels: "Is there envy among you?... Do you have an evil inclination?" Nevertheless, the extensive replies which he gave — "Did you descend to Egypt? Were you enslaved to Pharaoh?... Do you work?... Are you involved in business?..." — are not all relevant. Thus it appears that Moshe's intent is not merely that the Torah enables us to overcome the *yetzer hara,* but instead points to a subject of more general scope.

BUILDING A HOME FOR G-D The concept can be explained as follows: The Torah was given in order to bring to realization G-d's intent for the Creation: His desire for a dwelling in the lower worlds.[26] This purpose serves as the basis for the

---

24. *Siddur Tehillat HaShem,* p. 107. See also the allegory of Rabbi Akiva (*Berachos* 61a) which compares the Jews to fish and the Torah to water.
25. *Kiddushin* 30b.
26. *Midrash Tanchuma, Parshas Naso,* sec. 16; *Tanya,* ch. 36.

refutation of the angels' claim. For the law is[27] that when a person buys a field for the purpose of building a home, and the neighbor desires to use it as a field, the neighbor is not granted this privilege.

Similarly, the Jews use the Torah to build G-d's dwelling in the lower worlds. Therefore, they — and not the angels — are entitled to it.

This intent is reflected in Moshe's lengthy reply in which he reckons the various different challenging situations the Jews must confront, describing the environment — the lower realms — where G-d desired His dwelling to be constructed.

One might, however, ask: Why must G-d's dwelling be fashioned in the lower worlds? Let the Torah be given to the angels — for they are its neighbors — and let them create a dwelling for G-d in the upper worlds.

The resolution to this question depends on several fundamental concepts in Chassidic thought. The concept of a dwelling refers to a place for the revelation of G-d's essence. In our mortal sphere, it is in our own homes that we let down our inhibitions and let our real selves be known. Similarly, in the analogy, it is in our material world, G-d's dwelling, that His essence, who He really is, becomes manifest.

How does that essence become manifest? Because it is invested in the Torah and in the Jewish people. With regard to the Torah, our Sages explain[28] that the word *Anochi*, the first word of the Ten Commandments serves as an acronym for the Aramaic words meaning "I wrote down and gave over My soul." And with regard to the Jewish people, it is explained that every Jewish soul is "an

---

27. *Bava Metzia, loc. cit.; Rambam, loc. cit.,* 14:1; *Tur* and *Shulchan Aruch, loc. cit.:*26.
28. *Shabbos* 105a; *Likkutei Torah, Shlach,* p. 48d.

actual part of G-d."[29] The angels do not possess such spiritual power.

It is in our lowly material world that the essential G-dliness possessed by the Torah and the Jewish people becomes manifest. Appreciating G-dliness in this material world presents a twofold challenge — a challenge from without, for the material nature of the world appears to oppose G-dliness,[30] and a challenge from within, for every person possesses an evil inclination. These challenges can be overcome only by tapping the essential G-dly power within our souls. And conversely, it is only by confronting these challenges — as opposed to appreciating the revelations of G-dliness in the spiritual worlds — that the essential G-dliness in our souls can be revealed.

For this reason, the Torah was given in this world — to enable the Jewish people to transform the darkness of our world into a dwelling for G-d.[31]

---

29. *Tanya,* ch. 2.
30. To use terminology from *Chassidus (Tanya,* ch. 6): Our world is "filled with *kelipos* and the *sitra achra* which are directly opposed to G-d."
31. This transformation is a new development, reflecting as radical a metamorphosis as the creation of the world. G-d created the world *yesh me'ayin,* bringing existence into being from absolute nothingness. The Divine service of the Jewish people involves transforming *yesh* into *ayin,* making the material existence of this world into a medium for the revelation of G-dliness.

    This process of transformation is also alluded to in Moshe's question to the angels: "Do you have a mother and a father?" The power to create a new entity is within G-d's essence alone *(Tanya, Iggeres HaKodesh,* Epistle 20). This power He communicated to the Jewish people, and therefore it is within the potential of mankind to conceive children, thus bringing new life into the world.

ISSUES IN
HALACHAH

WHAT IS DEAREST TO G-D?

Adapted from *Likkutei Sichos,* Vol. XXVII, p. 133ff.;
Chiddushim U'Biurim BeShas, Vol. III, p. 42ff.

WHY THE *SHABBOS* LAWS BECOME SUSPENDED

When debating the rationale for the ruling that a threat to life supersedes the prohibition against doing labor on *Shabbos,* the *Talmud* states:[1]

> Rabbi Shimon ben Menasia says: "[It is written:][2] 'And the children of Israel will observe the *Shabbos.*' The Torah is saying that you may desecrate one *Shabbos* for a person so that he will be able to observe many *Shabbasos.*"...

Rav Yehudah said in the name of Shmuel: "If I were among [the Sages mentioned previously], I would have said that my [method of deriving this concept] is preferable to theirs. [I would explain

---

1. *Yoma* 85b.
2. *Shmos* 31:16.

that it is written:][3] "And you shall live through them [the *mitzvos*]," i.e., you should live through them, and not die because of them.

Rava said: "All [the methods of deriving this concept suggested by the other Sages] can be disputed. [The method suggested] by Shmuel cannot be disputed.... For all the [methods of derivation suggested by the others can be substantiated] when one is certain [that a life will be saved], but when there is a doubt, the matter is left unresolved. [With regard to the method suggested] by Shmuel, even when there is doubt, there is no dispute."

Our Sages agree that the *halachah* follows Rava who favors the method of derivation suggested by Shmuel. Nevertheless, we find that the later *halachic* authorities also quote Rabbi Shimon ben Menasia's statements. Indeed, in his *Sheiltos*,[4] Rav Achai Gaon mentions only the words of Rabbi Shimon ben Menasia. It is thus necessary to understand: What is the difference between these two approaches and why are they both cited by the later authorities?

| **CONTRASTS BETWEEN** | The classic gloss to the |
| **THE TWO APPROACHES** | *Sheiltos*, the *Emek Ha-* |

Shaaleh, explains that the Rav Achai Gaon cites Rabbi Shimon ben Menasia's words, because he follows the opinion of the *Halachos Gedolos*[5] which states that one must violate the *Shabbos* laws even to save a fetus. The prooftext cited by Shmuel reads: "You

---

3. *Vayikra* 18:5.
4. *Sheilta* 1.
5. Cited by the *Ramban* in his text, *Toras Adam,* and Rabbeinu Nissim and Rabbeinu Asher in their glosses to *Yoma,* ch. 8.

shall keep My statutes... which a man shall observe and live through them." A fetus cannot be considered a man. Hence, Shmuel's approach would not apply in this instance. The logic suggested by Rabbi Shimon ben Menasia, by contrast, that by desecrating one *Shabbos* on a person's behalf, one gives him the opportunity to observe many, would also apply in the case of a fetus.[6]

There is another difference between the two approaches. Shmuel's approach applies to the entire Torah. Whenever there is a threat to life, it supersedes all the laws of the Torah except the prohibitions against idol worship, murder, and forbidden sexual relations. Rabbi Shimon ben Menasia's approach, by contrast, specifically relates to the *Shabbos*. One *Shabbos* may be violated for the sake of others. Indeed, there are approaches which explain that Rabbi Shimon ben Menasia is concerned only with the observance of other *Shabbasos,* and when the person will certainly not live to observe other *Shabbasos,*

---

6. See also the commentaries to *Niddah 44b.*

The *Emek HaShaaleh* goes further and explains the precise wording of the *Halachos Gedolos:* "When there is a pregnant woman whom we know will miscarry [unless she eats], she may be given [food] on Yom Kippur," to imply that the license to violate a prohibition to save the life of the fetus is granted only when "we know," i.e., that the threat to life is certain. If, however, there is a doubt regarding the matter, license is not granted.

What is the rationale for that approach? Our Sages' statements (*Yoma, loc. cit.*) that Rabbi Shimon ben Menasia's approach does not grant license when there is doubt.

This approach is not, however, followed by other authorities. The *Ramban* and Rabbeinu Nissim maintain that even if there is merely a possible chance of saving the life of a fetus, one may transgress the *Shabbos* (or Yom Kippur) laws.

One may say, however, that their approach is a juxtaposition of both teachings. From Rabbi Shimon ben Menasia, they derive that one may violate the *Shabbos* laws to save the life of a fetus, and from Shmuel, they derive the concept that this license is granted even when there is no certainty regarding the matter.

even though he will live long enough to perform other *mitzvos,* his life should not be saved.[7]

Tosafos[8] states that even according to Rabbi Shimon ben Menasia's approach, the leniency is not restricted to enabling a person to observe other *Shabbasos* alone. Rather, the intent is that his life be saved so that he will be able to observe any other *mitzvos.*[9]

Nevertheless, even according to this conception, Rabbi Shimon ben Menasia places the emphasis on Torah observance. Why may the *Shabbos* laws be violated? Because the person will observe other *mitzvos* in the future. Shmuel, by contrast, operates from a different perspective. Life takes precedence over observance; the Torah and its *mitzvos* are means that enable the Jews to live in the most complete and fullest sense. When they do not lead to that purpose, they are overridden.[10]

Moreover, according to Rabbi Shimon ben Menasia's perspective, by violating the *Shabbos* laws to save a life, a

---

7.   *Or HaChayim, Shmos* 31:16.

8.   *Yoma, loc. cit.*

9.   See the *Chasam Sofer, Yoreh De'ah,* Responsum 245, which states that from Rabbi Shimon ben Menasia's teaching, we learn only that the *Shabbos* laws may be violated for the purpose of observing other *Shabbasos,* and not for the purpose of observing other *mitzvos.* Nevertheless, from this teaching, we can extrapolate and deduct that similarly other *mitzvos* can be violated to save a person's life and enable him to observe these *mitzvos* in the future. See also the discussion of the question by *Ohelei Yosef, Dinai Kiddush HaShem,* sec. 23:213.

10. See *Rashi, Yoma* 82a: "The rationale for this is: G-d cherishes the soul of a Jew more than all the *mitzvos.*"

     To refer to a parallel concept: *Tanna D'Bei Eliyahu* (ch. 14) states: "Two entities preceded the world: the Torah and the Jewish people. We do not know which came first. Since [the Torah] says: 'Speak to the children of Israel,' 'Say to the children of Israel,' we may assume the Jewish people came first." (See *Likkutei Sichos,* Vol. XXXIV, p. 22, fn. 48.)

person has desecrated the *Shabbos*. To be sure, the dese-cration is licensed — and indeed, commanded — but it is a negative act. According to Shmuel, by contrast, the person has followed the Torah's commandments, for first and foremost, the Torah teaches us "to live through them." Thus, as will be explained, violating the *Shabbos* laws in such an instance can be considered as observance of the *Shabbos*.

THE RAMBAM'S REDUNDANCY On this basis, we can understand a difficulty that arises with regard to the *Rambam's* treatment of this concept in his *Mishneh Torah*. In his *Hilchos Shabbos,* he writes:[11]

> [The laws of] the *Shabbos* are suspended in the face of a danger to life, as are [the obligations of] the other *mitzvos*. Therefore, we may do every-thing that is necessary for the sake of a person whose life is in danger.

And he continues:[12]

> It is forbidden to hesitate before transgressing the *Shabbos* [laws] on behalf of a person who is dan-gerously ill. This is reflected by the verse which states: "[You shall keep My statutes...] which a man shall observe and live through them." [We must "live through them,"] and not die through them.

This elaboration is seemingly unnecessary. In *Hilchos Yesodei HaTorah,*[13] the *Rambam* has already quoted this

---

11. *Mishneh Torah, Hilchos Shabbos,* 2:1.
12. *Ibid., Halachah 3.*
13. Ch. 5, *Halachah 1. Hilchos Yesodei HaTorah* is the very first set of laws in the *Mishneh Torah*. Having stated this principle in this source, it would seemingly be unnecessary for him to restate it again.

same prooftext to teach us that whenever presented with a challenge whether to violate a *mitzvah* rather than sacrifice our lives, we should violate the *mitzvah* with the exception of the three transgressions mentioned above. And he continues[14] to explain that the same principle applies with regard to treating illnesses. If it is necessary to violate a prohibition of the Torah to save a sick person's life, we must. Why then does the *Rambam* repeat these same concepts with regard to the *Shabbos* laws?[15]

A DIFFERENT FORM OF OBSERVANCE The rationale depends on the difference between the approach of Rabbi Shimon ben Menasia and Shmuel explained above. According to Shmuel, the violation of the *Shabbos* laws is not merely permitted; in this situation, it is the way the *Shabbos* must be observed.[16]

---

14. *Ibid., Halachah* 6.
15. In essence, the same question arises with regard to the passage in *Yoma* cited above. That passage begins: "What is the source [which teaches] that a threat to life supersedes the *Shabbos* laws?" Previously, in that very same tractate (82a), our Sages stated: "There is no *mitzvah* that stands in the face of a threat to life with the exception of idol worship, forbidden sexual relations, and murder." Why would anyone think that this concept would not apply with regard to the *Shabbos*? This leads to the conclusion that the passage comes to teach us a unique concept with regard to the *Shabbos* itself as will be explained.
16. It can be explained that this concept is highlighted by the context in which the *Rambam* mentions the prooftext "And you shall live with them," i.e., *Halachah* 3 in connection with the statement, "It is forbidden to hesitate before transgressing the *Shabbos* [laws] on behalf of someone who is dangerously ill."
    The commentaries explain that the *Rambam's* source is the *Jerusalem Talmud* (*Yoma* 8:5) which states that a person who asks whether the *Shabbos* laws should be broken is a murderer, while one who acts with haste is to be praised. The *Rambam* does not employ that wording, for it appears to imply that the emphasis is on saving a life over and above all *halachic* conditions. The wording employed by the *Ram-*

By restating the leniency regarding overriding the *Shabbos* laws in the face of a threat to life, the *Rambam* emphasizes that the prohibitions are lifted entirely, for in this instance, the observance of the *Shabbos* involves violating its laws.[17]

To explain: With regard to *Shabbos*, it is written:[18] "Keep my *Shabbasos*, for [the *Shabbos*] is a sign between Me and you." *Rashi* comments: "[The *Shabbos*] is a great sign between us, that I chose you, by giving you My day of rest as a day of rest for yourselves as a heritage."

When a Jew's life is in danger on *Shabbos*, and the *Shabbos* laws are violated to the save that Jew's life, we are affirming the covenant between G-d and the Jewish people. Overriding the *Shabbos* laws emphasizes that G-d has chosen the Jewish people and regards each one with special care. This is the same theme expressed by the observance of *Shabbos*. Thus in this instance, the violation of the *Shabbos* laws exemplifies the theme of the *Shabbos* itself.

Our Sages describe *Shabbos* as "a microcosm of the world to come." May our study and observance of the *Shabbos* laws lead to the coming of "the day which is all *Shabbos* and rest for life everlasting,"[19] with the coming of *Mashiach*.

---

bam, by contrast, indicates that violating the *Shabbos* laws on behalf of a sick person is a way of observing the *Shabbos*.

17. The *Rambam* states that this concept also applies to "[the obligations of] the other *mitzvos*." The *Rambam* does not state this in *Hilchos Yesodei HaTorah*, however, because this concept is derived from the laws of *Shabbos*.

18. *Shmos* 31:13.

19. Cf. the conclusion of tractate *Taanis*.

TO BE CONSUMED
BY THE ALTAR'S FIRE

Adapted from *Likkutei Sichos,* Vol. III,
Parshas Tzav, p. 948ff.

WHEN CAN OUR SAGES ENFORCE RESTRICTIONS?	On the verse:[1] "This is the law of the burnt offering.... [It shall remain on] the altar's hearth throughout the night," *Rashi*

comments: "This comes to teach that burning the fats and
limbs of the sacrifices is permitted throughout the night."
According to Scriptural law, an attempt should be made to
burn all the portions of the sacrifice during the day; this is
the desired time for this activity.[2] After the fact, however,
if the other services associated with the sacrifice were performed during the day, one may burn the fats and limbs at
night.

Our Sages[3] placed restrictions on several *mitzvos* fulfilled during the night. Although Scriptural law permits

---

1. *Vayikra* 6:2.
2. *Menachos* 72a; *Rambam, Mishneh Torah, Hilchos Maaseh HaKorbonos* 4:3.
3. *Berachos* 2a.

these activities until daybreak, our Sages required that they be performed before midnight in order to "place a distance between a person and sin."

There is a difference of opinion between the *Rambam* and *Rashi*[4] as to whether this decree was applied to the burning of sacrificial fats and limbs. The *Rambam* maintains[5] that the Sages included this in their restriction, while *Rashi* argues that the Sages left the Scriptural law unchanged.

Rashi's opinion can be explained on the basis of a distinction between the burning of fats and limbs and the other *mitzvos*. According to several authorities,[6] when the Torah explicitly states that an activity is permitted, our Sages cannot prohibit it. Since the Torah says the fats and limbs can be burnt "throughout the night," and states:[7] "Do not allow the fat of the festive offering to remain until morning," the Sages did not have the authority to institute a prohibition in this regard.

Following this logic, the *Rambam's* ruling becomes difficult to understand. Several *Acharonim* maintain that the *Rambam* accepts the above principle.[8] Why then does he

---

4. *Berachos, ibid.*
5. *Ibid.*, 4:2; *Hilchos Temidim U'Musafim* 1:6.
6. See *Turei Zahav, Orach Chayim*, the conclusion of sec. 588 (with regard to the observance of the *mitzvos*), and *Yoreh De'ah* 117:1 (with regard to optional activities). See also *S'dei Chemed, Kellalim, Maareches Yud*, secs. 17-27; *Darchei Teshuvah, Yoreh De'ah* 117:4, and others.

   It appears that the Alter Rebbe does not accept this principle, even with regard to a *mitzvah*, as reflected in *Shulchan Aruch HaRav* 588:4. There is room for further deliberation concerning this matter.
7. *Shmos* 23:18. As reflected in *Sefer HaChinuch (Mitzvah 90)*, this prohibition applies to all other sacrifices and to the portions of sacrifices which have to be burnt on the altar.
8. See *S'dei Chemed, loc. cit.*, sec. 17.

maintain that the Sages restricted the burning of the sacrificial limbs and fats to the hours before midnight?

| **Two Dimensions of the Consumption of a Sacrifice** | The *Rambam's* ruling can be explained as follows: On the verse,[9] "And if the meat of the peace offering is eaten on |

the third day," our Sages[10] note that the verb is repeated, האכל יאכל, and comment: "The verse is speaking about two types of 'eating' — consumption by man and consumption by the fire of the altar." On this basis, the *Talmud* develops a parallel between partaking of sacrificial meat and burning portions of the sacrifice on the altar.

With regard to consumption of the sacrifices by man, there is also a *mitzvah* that people should eat their portion of the offering "on the day it was sacrificed."[11] Thus, there are two dimensions to the human consumption of a sacrifice at the appropriate time:

a) The positive *mitzvah* of partaking of the sacrifice. This is reflected in the blessing recited before eating from an offering.[12]

b) Eating the sacrifice on the day it was offered precludes the transgression of *nosar*, leaving sacrificial meat until the following morning.

These two dimensions are not entirely matching. Several conditions must be met with regard to the priests' partaking of the sacrifices: e.g., they must be eaten in a

---

9.   *Vayikra* 7:18.
10. *Zevachim* 13b.
11. *Vayikra* 7:15. See *Rambam, Mishneh Torah, Hilchos Maaseh HaKorbonos* 10:7.
12. See the *Mishnah* and the *Tosefta* at the conclusion of *Pesachim*.

manner which befits people of stature;[13] they may not be eaten uncooked.[14] If these conditions are not met, one has not performed the *mitzvah.*

With regard to *nosar,* by contrast, it makes no difference how one partakes of the sacrifice; as long as the meat does not remain, one has not violated the prohibition.

Parallels to these two dimensions of the human consumption of sacrificial meat exist with regard to the consumption of the fats and limbs by the fire of the altar. Thus burning the fats and limbs of the sacrifice on the altar:

a) is one of the services involved in offering the sacrifices, contributing a positive quality;

b) precludes the sin of *nosar.*

Based on the above, it is possible to explain why, at the outset, one should burn the fats and limbs during the day, and only after the fact is it acceptable to burn them during the night. (Indeed, it is rare to find instances in which Scriptural law makes a distinction between "at the outset" (לכתחילה) and "after the fact" (בדיעבד).[15]) The positive dimension — burning the fats and limbs — must (like all other services associated with the sacrifices) be performed during the day. The license which the Torah

---

13. *Bamidbar* 18:8; *Zevachim* 91a. See the *Chacham Tzvi* (Responsum 62), who explains that this is a binding obligation.

14. The above enables us to understand the statement of *Tosafos* (*Menachos* 48a) that eating uncooked sacrificial meat is not considered a merit. Although one is permitted to eat sacrificial meat uncooked (as *Tosafos, loc. cit.* 99b proves), doing so is not considered a *mitzvah,* because this is not a proper way to eat sacrificial food. Although it precludes *nosar,* it is not considered a merit for an individual.

15. See the discussion of this concept in the works of R. Yosef Engel: *Lekach Tov* (sec. 5), *Asvin D'Oraisa,* sec. 12. See also *Darchei Sholom, Os Bet* (printed also in the Kehot edition of *S'dei Chemed,* p. 4258).

grants to burn the fats and limbs throughout the night is merely to prevent the sin of *nosar.*

Therefore, at the outset, the fats and the limbs must be burnt during the day as part of — and during the time set aside for — the service of offering the sacrifices. If that was not performed, the fats and the limbs must be burnt at night so that the prohibition against *nosar* will be observed.

This enables us to explain the ruling of the *Rambam* mentioned previously. The *Rambam* maintains — in contrast to the opinion of the *Turei Zahav*[6] — that the principle which holds that the Sages have no power to forbid something which the Torah permits applies only with regard to the observance of *mitzvos.* When the Torah explicitly states that a *mitzvah* should be performed, our Sages do not have the power to rule that it should not.

But when a *mitzvah* is not involved, (and burning the fats and limbs at night does not have the status of a *mitzvah*), the Sages do have the power to enforce a restriction. Although the Torah states that these activities can be performed throughout the night, our Sages restricted their performance to the hours before midnight.

DEDICATING OUR PLEASURE TO G-D   All the elements of sacrificial worship in the *Beis HaMikdash* have parallels in our own Divine service. Fat is an analogy for satisfaction.[16] And we are commanded:[17] "All the fat [should be offered] to G-d," implying that a Jew must anchor his powers of pleasure and satisfaction to G-dliness.

---

16. See *Gittin* 56b.
17. *Vayikra* 3:16.

One might think that this refers only to the pleasure derived from material things, for we are taught that one's involvement in material affairs should be "as if compelled by a demon."[18] But what could be wrong with deriving pleasure from the observance of *mitzvos* and other holy matters?

We can take a lesson from the burning of fats on the altar. Although partaking of the sacrifices is a *mitzvah,* we may not eat from them until we have seen to the burning of their fats. This teaches us that we can be sure of having fulfilled a *mitzvah* in the proper way only after we have given all our satisfaction (including that derived from the *mitzvah* itself) to G-d. When a person has not dedicated his satisfaction to G-d, it is possible that he is fulfilling the *mitzvah,* not because the *Shulchan Aruch* orders its observance, but because of the satisfaction it brings.

One must feel energy and vitality in the observance of the *mitzvos,* observing them not simply out of compulsion, but out of a genuine love for G-d. The fact that one is able to fulfill G-d's will should be a person's greatest source of pleasure. Nevertheless, this satisfaction should be a by-product of one's commitment to G-d, and not a goal in its own right.

Based on the above, we can also appreciate why the *mitzvah* of burning the sacrificial fats applies only during the day, and the burning of fats at night is only to compensate for not burning them earlier. With regard to our Divine service, "day" refers to the times when we are occupied with the study of Torah and the observance of *mitzvos,* as reflected in the analogy:[19] "A *mitzvah* is a candle, and the Torah, light." Night and darkness, by contrast,

---

18. *Nedarim* 20b; see also *Torah Or, Megillas Esther,* p. 93c.
19. *Mishlei* 6:23.

represent times when a person is not occupied with the Torah or its *mitzvos,* but with material concerns.

The lesson about dedicating the fat — our potential for pleasure and satisfaction — to G-d applies primarily during the day. When it comes to material things, it is obvious that a person should not seek his own pleasure, but should perform "all his deeds for the sake of Heaven."[20] When it comes to the Torah and its *mitzvos,* however, it is possible that a person might feel that his motives are not important; as long as he studies the Torah and performs its *mitzvos,* it is acceptable. And he will rationalize his behavior, quoting our Sages:[21] "A person should always occupy himself in the Torah and its *mitzvos...* [even] for a selfish intent."

Such a person has to be taught: The fats must first be offered on the altar. The very foundation of the Torah and its *mitzvos* is self-transcendence.

May our efforts to "burn the fats" — to rise above selfish forms of pleasure — during the night of exile, lead to the dawn of Redemption. Then the *Beis HaMikdash* will be rebuilt and we will again offer all the sacrifices. May this take place in the immediate future.

---

20. *Avos* 2:15.
21. *Pesachim* 50b. See *Shulchan Aruch HaRav, Hilchos Talmud Torah* 4:3, and the *Kuntres Acharon.*

THE RESPONSIBILITY FOR CHINUCH

Based on *Likkutei Sichos*, Vol. XVII,
Parshas Kedoshim, p. 233ff.; Vol. XXXV, p. 61ff.

WHO IS RESPONSIBLE	*Bar Mitzvah*, the Jewish term
FOR A CHILD'S	for coming of age, literally
OBSERVANCE?	means "one obligated to

fulfill the commandments."
Before *Bar Mitzvah,* a child also observes *mitzvos,* but this
observance is termed merely *chinuch,* "training," for the
child is considered to lack the maturity to accept the
responsibility for his Jewish practice.

Indeed, with regard to the observance of *mitzvos* as
chinuch, there is a difference of opinion among our Rabbis
regarding the extent of a child's responsibility. *Rashi*[1] and
the *Ramban*[2] maintain that the child is not responsible for
his observance even according to Rabbinic law. The obligation of *chinuch* is incumbent on the child's father; he

---

1. *Berachos* 48a.
2. *Milchamos HaShem, Berachos* 20b.

must train his child to observe, but the child himself has no obligation whatsoever.

Tosafos[3] and Rabbeinu Nissim[4] maintain, by contrast, that when a child comes to the age when he is fit to be educated, he himself becomes responsible — according to Rabbinic law — to observe these *mitzvos.*

To illustrate these contrasting views: According to Scriptural law, one is not required to recite the Grace After Meals unless one ate a portion of bread that is thoroughly satisfying. Our Sages, however, were stringent and imposed a requirement that Grace be recited as long as one has eaten an amount of bread equal to the volume of an olive. They also required a child to recite grace as *chinuch.*

One of the principles of Jewish law is that one who hears [a blessing] is considered as having recited it himself.[5] Thus one can fulfill one's obligation for grace by listening to it being recited by another person, provided that person is also obligated to recite grace.

An adult who has eaten to the point of satisfaction cannot fulfill his obligation to recite grace by listening to grace recited by a child, for the adult is obligated to recite grace by Scriptural law, and there is no such obligation incumbent on the child. The question arises, however, with regard to an adult who ate only a small portion of bread, and whose obligation is Rabbinic in origin. Can he fulfill his obligation by listening to grace recited by a child?

According to *Tosafos* and Rabbeinu Nissim, since the child is himself obligated by Rabbinic law to observe the *mitzvah,* an adult whose obligation is Rabbinic in origin

---

3.   *Berachos* 48a.
4.   *Megillah,* the conclusion of ch. 2.
5.   *Rambam, Mishneh Torah, Hilchos Berachos* 1:11.

can fulfill his obligation by listening to his blessings. The *Ramban* and others who follow his approach[6] do not allow a child to discharge an adult's responsibility, even if that responsibility is Rabbinic in origin. For they maintain that the child himself is not obligated at all; the obligation rests on his father.

| **WHAT IS THE RAMBAM'S VIEW?** The *Rambam* does not explicitly mention the above issue. Nevertheless, since he rules[7] that when a father has not eaten his fill, a son can discharge the obligation of grace on his behalf, we can assume that he follows the approach of *Tosafos* and Rabbeinu Nissim which maintains that the responsibility is the child's alone.

This concept is also reflected in the *Rambam's* wording in several sources. For example, in *Hilchos Tzitzis*,[8] he states: "According to Rabbinic law, a child who knows how to wrap himself [in a garment] is *obligated* [to wear] *tzitzis* to train him in the observance of the *mitzvos*." Similarly, in *Hilchos Berachos*,[9] he writes: "Minors are obligated by Rabbinic decree to recite grace to train them in the observance of the *mitzvos*." This choice of wording[10] indicates that the Sages placed the obligation on the child himself.

---

6. The *Rashba* and the *Ritba*, commentaries to *Sukkah* 38a. *Rashi*, nevertheless, departs from those who share this approach and allows a child to discharge an adult's obligations for Grace. See the discussion of his approach in *Yagdil Torah* (N.Y.), Iyar, 5737.
7. *Ibid.* 5:15-16; note, however, the gloss of the *Kessef Mishneh* who gives a different interpretation of the *Rambam's* ruling.
8. *Mishneh Torah, Hilchos Tzitzis,* 3:9.
9. *Mishneh Torah, Hilchos Berachos,* 5:1.
10. See also parallels in *Hilchos Sukkah* 6:1, *Hilchos Lulav* 7:19, and other sources within the *Mishneh Torah*.

CAN A CHILD BE GIVEN RESPONSIBILITY?	The approach of the *Rambam, Tosafos,* and Rabbeinu Nissim raises a

fundamental question: A child's coming of age is not merely a chronological phenomenon; it is a result of his achievement of a degree of intellectual and emotional maturity. Until he reaches that age, he is unable to take responsibility for his conduct, and afterwards, he is considered mature enough to do so. How, then, can the Sages impose responsibility on him? To refer to an expression of the *Talmud:* "Can a child be held responsible to fulfill an obligation?"[11]

VIRTUE BY ASSOCIATION	This question can be answered through the introduction of a related

concept. Our Sages discuss the concept of *machshirei mitzvah,* the performance of tasks that are necessary to enable a *mitzvah* to be performed. For example, if a child must be circumcised on *Shabbos,* and there is not a proper knife available, Rabbi Eliezer permits one to carry a knife through the public domain (even though this violates the prohibitions against labor on the *Shabbos*).[12] And furthermore, he even permits a knife to be fashioned. For according to his opinion, just as the performance of the *mitzvah* itself supersedes the *Shabbos* laws, so, too, does the performance of any activity necessary to enable that *mitzvah* to be performed. Although Rabbi Eliezer's opinion is not accepted as *halachah,* even the Sages who differ do attach a measure of importance to *machshirei mitzvah.*

---

11. *Pesachim* 116a; see also *Tziyunim LiTorah, Klal* 12.
12. *Shabbos* 130a.

To cite another example: The *Jerusalem Talmud*[13] states that before building a *sukkah* or making a *lulav,* one should recite a blessing praising G-d for "sanctifying us with His commandments and commanding us to make a *sukkah*" or "a *lulav.*" Although the *mitzvah* is to dwell in the *sukkah* or to take the *lulav,* since it is impossible to fulfill that *mitzvah* without first making the *sukkah* or the *lulav,* the preliminary activity is important enough to warrant the recitation of a blessing.

The extension of the scope of a *mitzvah* applies also to people as well as to activities. For example, a person who is not capable of studying the Torah on an advanced level should set aside a certain amount of time every day for Torah and devote the majority of his efforts to earning a livelihood, supporting not only himself and his own family, but other Torah scholars,[14] giving them the opportunity to study the entire day.[15] The person who supports the scholars is given a share of their merit, and it is considered as if he studied himself.

To cite an even further extension of this concept: Women are not obligated to study the Torah. Nevertheless, if they help their husbands and sons to study, they

---

13. *Berachos* 9:3. Note also the discussion of this concept in *Likkutei Sichos,* Vol. XVII, p. 187ff.

14. See *Shulchan Aruch* and *Ramah, Yoreh De'ah* 246:1; *Shulchan Aruch HaRav, Hilchos Talmud Torah* 3:4.

15. A distinction can be made between the example mentioned above and the classic partnership between Yissachar and Zevulun. The reason Zevulun is given a share of Yissachar's merit is that, as *Shulchan Aruch HaRav* explains, the merit was earned by Yissachar, and is his to share if he desires. In contrast, in the example mentioned above, since the person is unable to study and he provides for the Torah study of others, G-d grants him a share in the Torah study of those individuals, independent of the person's decision.

are given a share in the performance of that *mitzvah*,[16] for
it is their assistance that makes this study possible.[17]

SHARING AN OBLIGATION The above concepts can also be related
to the *mitzvah* of *chinuch*. It can be
explained that the *mitzvah* is
incumbent on the father. Nevertheless, the child is an
active partner in the *mitzvah,* for after all, the father's
mitzvah involves the child's observance. It is not merely,
as in the instances mentioned above, that without the
child, the father could not observe the *mitzvah* of *chinuch,*
but that the *mitzvah* incumbent on the father is that his
child should perform *mitzvos*. And so, as a result of the
father's obligation, the child is also considered obligated.[18]

To explain the concept from a slightly different van-
tage point: Since the father is obligated to train his child in
the observance of the *mitzvos,* there is an obligation
binding the child to observance. Although it is the father's
mitzvah that requires him to observe, the child can still be
considered as obligated.

To cite a parallel: Our Sages[19] state that a woman is
obligated in the *mitzvah* of bringing festive peace offerings
on the three pilgrimage festivals. Rabbeinu Tam[20] explains

---

16. *Sotah* 21a; *Ramah, loc. cit.*:6; *Shulchan Aruch HaRav, loc. cit.,* the conclusion of ch. 1.
17. To cite another parallel: As Rabbeinu Nissim (in his commentary to
Kiddushin, the beginning of ch. 2) explains, the commandment to "be
fruitful and multiply" is incumbent upon males. Nevertheless, a
woman who gives birth "is also considered to have earned a *mitzvah,*
because she assists her husband in the fulfillment of his *mitzvah."*
18. See *S'dei Chemed, Klallim, Maareches Ches, Klal* 60, who explains that
the obligation the Sages placed on the father causes the child to also
be considered as obligated by Rabbinic law.
19. *Chagigah* 6a.
20. *Tosafos, Rosh HaShanah* 6b.

that the obligation to bring a festive peace offering is incumbent on the husband. Nevertheless, since the husband's rejoicing must encompass his entire household, a woman is also considered obligated[21] with regard to this sacrifice.[22]

Another more telling illustration of this principle can be seen from another ruling by the *Rambam*. In *Hilchos Talmud Torah*,[23] the *Rambam* writes: "[A child] who was not taught [Torah] by his father is obligated to teach himself when he appreciates [the importance of knowledge]." Noting that the *Rambam* uses the term "when he appreciates," and not "when he attains majority," the *Tzemach Tzedek*[24] writes — in wonder — that it appears that the *Rambam* maintains that there is an obligation on the child.

Based on the above principle, we can appreciate the *Rambam's* ruling. The *mitzvah* incumbent on the father is

---

21. The *Rambam, Mishneh Torah, Hilchos Chagigah* 1:1, rules that a woman is obligated in the *mitzvah* of bringing this festive peace sacrifice. It is possible to postulate that the *Rambam* follows the same logic as *Tosafos,* and that the positions of these two authorities with regard to the festive peace offerings parallel their views with regard to *chinuch.* In both instances, since the *mitzvah* incumbent on one person requires that another become an active partner in the effort, the partner is also considered as obligated.

22. To cite another example: the *mitzvah* of *yibbum,* the obligation incumbent on the brother of a man who died childless to marry the widow of his deceased brother. Although the *mitzvah* is incumbent on the brother, it also encompasses the widow. She is also considered as "obligated."

On that basis, the *Haflaah* (notes to *Kiddushin* 24b) states that it is a *mitzvah* for the Jews to receive the Priestly Blessing. Although the Torah command is directed only to the priests who give the blessing, when there are no Jews to bless, the priests cannot perform their *mitzvah.* Therefore, the recipients of the blessing are also considered to be involved in a *mitzvah.*

23. *Mishneh Torah, Hilchos Talmud Torah* 1:3.

24. *Piskei Dinim, Chiddushim al HaRambam.*

"And you shall teach them diligently to your children,"[25] requiring the child's active involvement. Accordingly, the obligation of that *mitzvah* is also extended to include the child as well.[26]

On the verse:[27] "Set up marking posts for yourselves," the *Ramban*[28] explains that the *mitzvos* we observe in the present era are merely preparatory steps, *chinuch,* for the ultimate observance of the *mitzvos* which will take place in the Era of the Redemption. They prepare not only ourselves, but also the world at large, readying it for that ultimate era; may it come soon.

---

25. *Devarim* 6:7.
26. This is a greater inclusion, for in contrast to *chinuch,* which is a Rabbinic command, the commandment to study the Torah is Scriptural in origin. Thus, according to the *Tzemach Tzedek's* interpretation of the *Rambam's* ruling, the Torah itself is placing an obligation on a child.
27. *Yirmeyahu* 31:20.
28. *Vayikra* 18:25.

SHOULD WE RESTRICT THE AMOUNT WE GIVE?

Adapted from *Likkutei Sichos*, Vol. XXVII, p. 217ff.;
Chiddushim U'Biurim BeShas, Vol. III, p. 152ff.

| AN APPARENT CONTRADICTION | In the *Mishneh Torah*, the *Rambam* writes:[1] |

A person should never consecrate or dedicate all of his property. Indeed, a person who does so violates the Torah's intent, for it is written:[2] "[Any dedication which a person will dedicate to G-d] from all that he possesses...." [The Torah states:] "from all," i.e., not all.

[When a person gives all his property away], our Sages[3] termed this foolishness, and not piety. For he forfeits all his assets, and will need the assis-

---

1. *Hilchos Erachin VeCharamim* 8:13.
2. *Vayikra* 27:28.
3. *Erachin* 28a.

tance of others. One should not have mercy upon
him.

With regard to such individuals, our Sages said:[4]
"Men of foolish piety are among those who destroy
the world." Instead, one who distributes his
wealth... should not distribute more than a fifth.

In his *Commentary to the Mishnah,*[5] the *Rambam*
appears to follow a different perspective. On the teaching:
"These are the precepts for which no fixed measure is
prescribed," he writes:

This — that deeds of kindness have no fixed measure — refers to helping a person with one's efforts.
There is a measure, however, with regard to helping a person financially: one fifth of one's
resources. A person should not obligate himself to
give more than a fifth of his resources *unless he
does so as an expression of piety.*

Thus, in his *Commentary to the Mishnah,* although the
Rambam advises that a person's gifts should not exceed a
fifth of his resources, he does not restrict one to that
measure. If a person desires to act piously, he may exceed
that limit. In the *Mishneh Torah,* by contrast, the *Rambam*
states unequivocally that a person's gifts should not
exceed a fifth.

| **TWO DIFFERENT** | It is, however, possible to explain |
| **TYPES OF GIVING** | this difference[6] as follows:[7] In his |

---

4. *Sotah* 20a.
5. *Peah* 1:1.
6. The *Mishneh Torah* is a later work than the *Commentary on the Mish-
    neh* and thus it contains several rulings in which the *Rambam* reverses
    a position which he held previously. Nevertheless, by and large, there
    is a consistency in the *Rambam's halachic* judgments.

Commentary to the Mishnah, the *Rambam* is speaking about a situation of immediate and apparent need; there are captives to ransom, hungry people to feed, or needy to clothe. In such an instance, although one is not obligated to give more than a fifth, one may do so if one desires. In his *Mishneh Torah,* by contrast, the *Rambam* is speaking of a person dedicating his property for charitable purposes, but not necessarily meeting situations of immediate need. In such a circumstance, it is improper to give away more than a fifth.

This interpretation is reflected in the context in which the *Rambam's* rulings were given. In describing the value of the gifts and consecrated property mentioned in *Hilchos Erachin VeCharamim,* the *Rambam* writes:[8] "It is proper for a person to practice such generosity [so as] to influence his [natural] inclination, [so that] he will not be miserly," i.e., the purpose of such gifts are not to meet the needs of others,[9] but rather to shape one's own character. For this purpose, it is not proper to give more than a fifth.

The *Commentary to the Mishneh,* by contrast, is speaking about deeds of kindness and charity, of which the *Rambam* writes:[10] "It is a positive commandment to give charity to the poor according to what is appropriate for him [the recipient]." This indicates that the emphasis is on the needs of the poor person, and if another person has the means, he should endeavor to meet the poor

---

7. See *Birchai Yosef, Yoreh De'ah* 249:1, and the *Beis Din Shel Shlomo, Yoreh De'ah,* Responsum 1.

8. *Mishneh Torah, Hilchos Erachin VeCharamim* 8:12.

9. In that context, it is significant to note that in *Hilchos Erachin VeCharamim,* the *Rambam* mentions dedications to the *Beis HaMikdash* and the like, but not gifts to charity.

10. *Mishneh Torah, Hilchos Matanos Aniyim* 7:1.

man's needs, even if this requires him to give away more than a fifth of his resources.[11]

REDEEMING ONE'S SOUL   In *Tanya, Iggeres HaTeshuvah,*[12] the Alter Rebbe states:

A person may redeem his fasts[13] with charity.... Although this may amount to a considerable sum, he need not fear [violation of] the injunction: "Do not distribute more than a fifth." For giving for these reasons is not considered "distributing," since he is giving to release himself from fasting and affliction. This is no less necessary than medication for his body or any of his other needs.

Similarly, in *Iggeres HaKodesh,*[14] the Alter Rebbe states:
The ruling: "One who distributes should not distribute more than a fifth," applies only to one who has not sinned, or has atoned for his sins through penances and fasts.... But he who has yet to correct his soul's [blemishes, he should give] surely. For the healing of the soul is not less important than the healing of the body, for which money is no

---

11. In *Hilchos Matanos Aniyim* 7:5, the *Rambam* also mentions the measure of one fifth. He does not, however, state that it is forbidden to give in excess of this measure, for he is speaking about meeting the immediate needs of the poor.

    See also *Shailis Yaavetz,* Responsum 3; see also the letter of the Rebbe Rashab (printed in *Sefer HaMaamarim 5709,* p. 21): "The *mitzvah* of charity has no measure as the *Shulchan Aruch, Yoreh De'ah* 249:1 says: 'The measure of charity is according to the needs of the poor,'" i.e., it is unlimited.

12. The conclusion of ch. 3.

13. I.e., those fasts required as penance for sins.

14. Epistle 10.

object, as it is written:[15] "All that a man has, he will give on behalf of his soul."

It must be emphasized that from a strict *halachic* perspective, the Alter Rebbe may rule even more strictly than the *Rambam*. For it appears[16] that he follows the opinion of the *Ramah*[17] who rules that it is forbidden to distribute more than one fifth of one's resources to charity even when a direct need is involved. Indeed, this is evident from the Alter Rebbe's wording itself: "He need not fear [violation of] the injunction: 'Do not distribute more than a fifth.'" This implies that were a person not concerned with cleansing his soul of spiritual blemishes, he should follow the injunction not to distribute more than a fifth.

Why then does the Alter Rebbe advise giving more than a fifth? Not because the immediate needs of the people are pressing as the *Rambam* maintains, but to enable a person to remove the blemishes from his soul. For just as a person will spend unlimitedly to care for his physical health, so too, he may spend unlimitedly to care for his spiritual health.

*   *   *

It is within the potential of *tzedakah,* not only to remove undesirable spiritual influences, but more importantly, to precipitate the revelation of positive ones. Thus our Sages state:[18] "Great is *tzedakah* for it brings the Redemption near," hastening the time when "there will be neither famine... for good things will flow in abundance

---

15. *Iyov* 2:4.
16. See the *Shulchan Aruch HaRav, Hilchos Mechirah, Kuntres Acharon,* law 4.
17. *Yoreh De'ah* 249:1.
18. *Bava Basra* 10a.

and all the delights will be as freely available as dust,"[19] with the coming of *Mashiach;* may this take place in the immediate future.

❦

---

19. *Rambam, Mishneh Torah, Hilchos Melachim* 12:5.

ACCEPTING RESPONSIBILITY FOR ANOTHER PERSON

Adapted from *Likkutei Sichos,* Vol. XXVI, p. 145ff.

THE PERSPECTIVE OF THE BABYLONIAN TALMUD The concluding *mishnah* in the tractate of *Bava Basra* states:[1]

When a guarantor is designated after a contract of a loan is signed, [the lender] may collect the debt from the property [possessed by the guarantor].[2]

An incident occurred, and Rabbi Yishmael ruled that [the lender] may collect the debt from the property [possessed by the guarantor].

Ben Nannas told him: He may collect neither from property which [the guarantor] has sold, nor from property in his possession.

"Why not?" he asked.

---

1. 175b.
2. In contrast to property which he sold.

He answered him: "If an individual would be strangling a colleague in the street and another person
would come and say 'Release him, and I will pay
you,' [the latter] would not be held liable, for [the
lender] did not give the money because of [the
guarantor's] faithfulness.

"What is an instance where a guarantor would be
held liable? When he said: 'Lend him money, and I
will pay you.' He is liable, because [the lender]
gave the loan because of [the guarantor's] faithfulness."

Rabbi Yishmael said: "...A person who desires to
involve himself with monetary law should serve
Shimon ben Nannas."

The *Gemara* states[3] that although Rabbi Yishmael
praised Shimon ben Nannas, he did not retract his own
view. And indeed, the *halachah* follows Rabbi Yishmael's
approach. The *Gemara* then asks: "What is the law when
one is strangling another person?" and replies, "Rabbi
Yishmael differs also with regard to a person who is strangling a colleague and the *halachah* follows his approach in
this instance as well."

The *Gemara,* however, concludes by explaining that
when someone is being strangled by his creditor and
another person volunteers to pay his debt so that the
creditor will release him, the guarantor becomes liable if
he performs a *kinyan,* an act of contract which affirms his
commitment.[4] Summing up the matter, the *Gemara* states:[5]

3.　176a.

4.　Our argument (throughout the essay) follows the interpretation of the
　　Shitah Mekubetzes (the conclusion of *Bava Basra*) which maintains that
　　according to Rabbi Yishmael, a *kinyan* is not necessary. It must be

The *halachah* is: A guarantor who makes a commitment when the money is given need not affirm his commitment with a *kinyan*. After the money is given, he must affirm his commitment with a *kinyan*.

Thus, when one person is strangling another, it is only when the guarantor affirms his commitment with a *kinyan* that his pledge is binding.

| **THE PERSPECTIVE OF THE** **JERUSALEM TALMUD** | The *Jerusalem Talmud* reviews the same *mishnah* and concludes as |

follows:

Rabbi Yeisa says in the name of Rabbi Yochanan: "Although Rabbi Yishmael praised ben Nannas, he praised him for his analogy, but the *halachah* does not follow ben Nannas."

Shimon bar Vavvah said in the name of Rabbi Yishmael: "Even in an instance where one person is strangling another, the *halachah* follows Rabbi Yishmael."

Rabbi Yossi says: "From this we understand that if one person ambushes a colleague in the marketplace and another person comes and says: 'Let him go and I will pay,' he should collect from the latter and not from the former."

---

noted, however, that the *Rambam* (in his *Commentary to the Mishnah*), the *Nimukei Yosef,* and others maintain that Rabbi Yishmael also requires a *kinyan* for an obligation on the guarantor to be binding. According to this approach, ben Nannas, by contrast, maintains that a guarantor is not liable even if he affirms his commitment with a *kinyan.*

5.   *Ibid.*:b.

Thus unlike the *Babylonian Talmud*, the *Jerusalem Talmud* does explicitly stipulate that a *kinyan* is necessary for the guarantor to become liable.

The wording of the *Jerusalem Talmud's* conclusion: "he should collect from the latter and not from the former" is, however, difficult to understand. For there is no logic to say that the guarantor's obligation should be stronger than that of the borrower, and that payment should be requested from him and not from the borrower.[6]

Because of this difficulty, the *P'nei Moshe*[7] interprets the final phrase as a rhetorical question: "Should he collect from the latter and not from the former?" According to this interpretation, by requesting the attacker to release his victim, the person is not necessarily undertaking a serious commitment as a guarantor. Instead, he is concerned with saving the life of the victim. According to this explanation, the *Jerusalem Talmud* follows the same reasoning as the *Babylonian Talmud,* and when a person saves a colleague from being attacked by committing himself to pay the debt, he is not held liable unless he affirms his word with a *kinyan*.

This interpretation is, however, difficult to accept. The difficulty cited by the *Pnei Moshe* is so obvious, that it is not necessary to negate it. Moreover, according to the conception of the *Pnei Moshe*, Rabbi Yossi is merely restating the position of ben Nannas in the *mishnah* without adding a new concept.

Thus it is more appropriate to say that Rabbi Yossi's statements should be interpreted in the context of the

---

6.   See *Bava Basra* 173a-b; *Rambam, Mishneh Torah, Hilchos Malveh ViLoveh,* ch. 25, *Tur* and *Shulchan Aruch,* sec. 129.

7.   One of the authoritative commentaries on the *Jerusalem Talmud,* whose gloss is printed on the same page as the text of the *Jerusalem Talmud,* as *Rashi's* commentary accompanies the *Babylonian Talmud.*

Jerusalem Talmud's position that the *halachah* follow Rabbi Yishmael's approach. As will be explained, his wording enables us to understand why a person making such a commitment would be obligated although he does not affirm his statements with a *kinyan*.

| **THE MOTIVATING** | To understand the differences in |
| **PRINCIPLES** | the positions of the *Babylonian* |

and *Jerusalem Talmuds,* it is necessary to focus on the fundamental rationale for a guarantor's obligation. After all, since he did not receive the loan himself, why should he be obligated to pay?

We find two rationales given by the *Babylonian Talmud:*

a) "The satisfaction which he derives from being accepted as a faithful person causes him to commit himself and undertake the obligation."[8]

b) "The lender could tell the guarantor: 'If it wasn't for you, I would not have given him a loan at all.'"[9]

According to the first interpretation, the guarantor's obligation comes as a result of the satisfaction he received. Receiving this satisfaction thus resembles a transaction which is itself a *kinyan,* and therefore no other *kinyan* is necessary.

According to the second interpretation, the guarantor's obligation does not stem from the satisfaction he received,

---

8. *Bava Basra* 173b. See the gloss of the *Ritva* which emphasizes this rationale.
9. *Bava Basra* 174a. See the glosses of Rabbeinu Gershom and the *Nimukei Yosef* which place the emphasis on this rationale. The *Nimukei Yosef* explains that the reason mentioned previously is important only to explain why the guarantor's commitment is not considered as an *asmachta,* a commitment which one never seriously intended to fulfill.

but rather stems from the fact that the lender undertook an expense because of him.[10] The fact that the lender relied on the guarantor and gave a loan because of his pledge is sufficient to motivate the guarantor to make a genuine commitment which he is obligated to uphold.

APPRECIATING THE DIFFERENCES IN APPROACH

A distinction between these two rationales can be seen in the case mentioned above, in which a person stops a lender from attacking a delinquent borrower by committing himself to pay the debt. The opinion that maintains that the guarantor's obligations stems from the lender spending money because of the guarantor's pledge would not hold the guarantor liable unless he affirms his commitment with a *kinyan*. For in this instance, the money had already been advanced, and the guarantor's commitment did not cause the lender to undertake any new expense.

The opinion which maintains that the guarantor's obligation stems from the satisfaction he received, by contrast, leads to a different conclusion. For in this instance, he did receive satisfaction — perhaps greater satisfaction for a person under attack was released because of him — and this is sufficient to cause him to make a binding commitment.

WHY THE TWO TALMUDS DIFFER?

On this basis, we can explain the difference in the approach

---

10. The intent is not that it is as if the guarantor caused the lender a loss, and he is liable to pay him damages (to cite a parallel: a person who shows a coin to a moneychanger and the moneychanger errs in quoting its value). Instead, the liability comes because of the guarantor's initiative. That initiative, however, is prompted by the fact that the other person undertook an expense because of him.

of the *Babylonian* and *Jerusalem Talmuds.* The *Babylonian Talmud* follows the second rationale mentioned above, that the guarantor's commitment stems from the fact that the lender advanced money because of him. Therefore, in the case of a guarantor who saves a person from being attacked by the lender, since the guarantor is not causing the lender any monetary loss, the guarantor's commitment must be affirmed by a *kinyan* to be binding.[11]

The *Jerusalem Talmud,* by contrast, accepts the first rationale, that the satisfaction the guarantor receives is sufficient to obligate him. Such satisfaction is also received when he saves a colleague from attack, and therefore he becomes liable.

This explanation allows for a new interpretation of Rabbi Yossi's words at the conclusion of the *Jerusalem Talmud:*

> "From this we understand that if one person ambushes a colleague in the marketplace and another person comes and says: 'Let him go and I will pay,' [he becomes liable, because now] he can collect from the latter and not from the former."

With these words, Rabbi Yossi is explaining why a guarantor becomes liable. The lender still retains his right to collect the debt from the borrower,[12] but at present it is

---

11. For according to the *Babylonian Talmud,* the satisfaction received by a person from the fact that he is considered faithful enough to repay a debt is not sufficient to create a binding obligation. When, however, a person is appointed as a guarantor by the court, the appointment is more distinguished and conveys a greater measure of satisfaction. Therefore, it is a sufficient to generate a binding obligation *(Rambam, loc. cit.:2).*

12. If this were not the case, the person making the commitment would not be considered as a guarantor, but rather as a person undertaking an independent commitment. See the commentaries of the *Meiri* and the *Ritbah* to this passage.

impossible for him to exercise that right (because the borrower is unable to pay). When the guarantor makes a
commitment that enables him to collect his debt from
him, this causes the lender to temporarily release the borrower from pressure, "[because now] he can collect from
the latter and not from the former." The satisfaction this
generates for the guarantor is sufficient to cause him to
make a binding commitment.

WHAT MOTIVATES THESE DIFFERENT APPROACHES? It is possible to explain that the
reason the *Jerusalem Talmud*
accepts a more encompassing
approach to the obligations of a
guarantor is that the concepts of unity and mutual responsibility share an intrinsic relationship with *Eretz Yisrael*,
the land in which the *Jerusalem Talmud* was authored.

To explain: The concept of mutual responsibility, *areivus*, that every Jew shares in the accountability for the
deeds of each member of our people, began with the entry
of the Jewish people into *Eretz Yisrael*.[13] At that time, the
Jewish people became a single communal entity, and not
merely a collection of individuals.[14]

This concept of mutual responsibility was perpetuated
even after the Jewish people were exiled. Therefore,
wherever they are located, one Jew can fulfill the responsibility of another Jew with regard to certain matters, e.g.,
the recitation of a blessing before performing a *mitzvah*.[15]
Nevertheless, the true sense of community exists only in
Eretz Yisrael. For this reason, the complete *halachic* defi-

---

13. *Sanhedrin* 43b; see *Rashi, Devarim* 29:28.
14. See the gloss of the Rogatchover Gaon to *Sanhedrin, loc. cit.*
15. *Rashi, Rosh HaShanah* 29a; *Shulchan Aruch HaRav*, the conclusion of sec. 167.

nition of a communal fast does not apply in the Diaspora, only in *Eretz Yisrael*.[16] For only in *Eretz Yisrael,* do the Jews function as a communal entity in the full sense.

The macrocosm is reflected in the microcosm. Because *Eretz Yisrael* is more closely related to the concept of mutual responsibility, when considering the idea of *areivus* in a financial sense, the Sages of *Eretz Yisrael* were willing to accept the concept even when it is not reinforced by deed. The satisfaction which a person receives is sufficient to bring about such an obligation. In Babylonia, by contrast, since the concept of mutual responsibility received less of an emphasis, the Sages required that a person perform an act, a *kinyan,* to reaffirm his commitment and cause it to become binding.

* * *

May the mutual responsibility our people share soon come to its most complete expression, when, with togetherness and unity, "a great congregation will return here,"[17] to *Eretz Yisrael,* with the coming of *Mashiach.* May this take place in the immediate future.

16. *Pesachim* 54b.
17. *Yirmeyahu* 31:8.

SPREADING TORAH KNOWLEDGE

Adapted from *Chiddushim U'Biurim BeShas,*
Vol. II, p. 167ff.

NEIGHBORLY	In *Hilchos Talmud Torah,*[1] the *Rambam*
CONDUCT	writes:

When there is a teacher of young children, and a colleague comes and opens a school to teach children next to him to attract other children, or even to attract the children [who are studying under the first teacher], [the first teacher] may not lodge a protest against him, as it is written:[2] "G-d desired for the sake of [Israel's] righteousness to make the Torah great and glorious."

The commentaries note that the apparent source for the *Rambam's* ruling is *Bava Basra* 21b-22a. That source, however, uses a different rationale, stating: "The envy of the scribes increases wisdom."

---

1. The conclusion of ch. 2.
2. *Yeshayahu* 42:21.

219

The *Rambam* frequently will quote a prooftext or rationale other than that used in his source,[3] for the *Rambam* quotes the rationale or prooftext which is most obvious and easily understood.

This reflects the goal stated by the *Rambam* in the introduction to the *Mishneh Torah:* "to compose clear statements.... using precise and succinct wording... so that all the laws [of the Torah] would be revealed for the great and the small." For this reason, the *Rambam* will change the wording in his statement of a law from that in his source, and similarly, he will — as in the instance above — offer a rationale that is more explicit than the one quoted in the original source.

SPEAKING WITHIN CONTEXT   The question arises: In the instance mentioned above, if the prooftext quoted by the *Rambam* is preferable to the rationale stated in the *Talmud,* why was it not employed by the Sages of the *Talmud?* One might say, based on the principle:[4] "The scholars of a later generation must explain their words more," that since the *Rambam* was writing to later generations of scholars, it was necessary for him to be more explicit. This statement itself, however, requires explanation: How is the prooftext quoted by the *Rambam* more explicit than the rationale employed by our Sages?

It is possible to explain that the difference between the two sources depends on the context in which they are speaking. The *Talmud* is speaking within the context of the laws of usurping a colleague's livelihood. It explains that although there are certain restrictions against open-

3.   *Yad Malachi, Klallei Rambam,* sec. 4.
4.   *Ibid.,* sec. 24; *Beis Yosef, Yoreh De'ah,* 201.

ing up a business in a place where a colleague already operates a similar business, these restrictions do not apply with regard to Torah instruction. Why? Because "The envy of the scribes increases wisdom," i.e., even the person who was teaching previously will benefit from the competition, for he will gain — and thus impart — greater knowledge.

The *Rambam,* by contrast, is speaking within the context of the *mitzvah* to teach the Torah to children. He concludes that concept by stressing the importance of the proliferation of Torah schools, stating that even when there is an existing school, another may be started. The prooftext he cites to illustrate this concept: "G-d desired for the sake of [Israel's] righteousness to make the Torah great and glorious," emphasizes the worthiness of such study in G-d's eyes, thus encouraging people to undertake such endeavors:

*   *   *

May the envy and competition in the teaching and the study of the Torah in the present era lead to the age when "there is neither envy nor competition... and the occupation of the entire world will be solely to know G-d,"[5] with the coming of *Mashiach;* may this take place in the immediate future.

---

5.   *Rambam, Mishneh Torah, Hilchos Melachim* 12:4.

HOW WE CAN FULFILL THE FINAL *MITZVAH* OF THE TORAH

Adapted from *Likkutei Sichos,*
Vol. XXIII, p. 17ff.; Vol. XXIV, p. 207ff.

AN OBVIOUS DIFFICULTY The *Rambam* writes:[1] It is a positive commandment incumbent on each and every Jewish man to write a Torah scroll for himself, as it is written:[2] "And now write down this song for yourself." [Implied is the commandment to] write [the entire] Torah which contains this song,[3] for the Torah should not be written down passage by passage.

Even though a person's ancestors left him a Torah scroll, it is a *mitzvah* for him to write [one] by him-

---

1. *Mishneh Torah, Hilchos Tefillin, U'Mezuzah V'Sefer Torah* 7:1.
2. *Devarim* 31:19.
3. I.e., and not merely the song *Haazinu* itself.

self. If he writes [a scroll] by hand, it is considered as if he received [the Torah] on Mount Sinai. If a person does not know how to write, others should write [the scroll] for him.

Anyone who checks even a single letter of a Torah scroll is considered as if he wrote the entire scroll.

The *Rambam's* words are also quoted by the *Shulchan Aruch.*[4] Nevertheless, in practice, it is not common to see individuals writing Torah scrolls. Although the *Rambam* considers this one of the *mitzvos* which a person must actively seek to fulfill,[5] the large majority of individuals — including even those who are punctilious regarding their observance of other commandments, do not seek to write a Torah scroll themselves.[6]

One might say that since most people are unable to write a Torah scroll properly, rather than fulfill the *mitzvah* themselves, they should commission a scribe to do so. For based on the verse,[7] "This is my G-d and I will glorify Him," our Sages state[8] that *mitzvos* must be performed in the most attractive and becoming way possible.[9]

---

4. *Yoreh De'ah* 270:1.
5. See *Sefer HaMitzvos,* the conclusion of the positive commandments.
6. Note the *Daas Kedoshim* and others who raise this question.
7. *Shmos* 15:2.
8. *Shabbos* 132b.
9. There is a principle in Torah law *(Kiddushin* 41a) that it is a greater *mitzvah* for a person to observe a *mitzvah* himself rather than entrust its performance to an agent. Thus one might think that for this reason, it would be preferable to write a Torah scroll oneself rather than entrust the writing of it to a scribe.

    Nevertheless, in this instance, this logic does not apply. The reason why it is preferable for a person to perform a *mitzvah* himself is that generally, by entrusting its performance to an agent, he implies that he does not want to trouble himself to perform the *mitzvah* himself. He is thus diminishing the honor of the *mitzvah*.

This, however, merely shifts the emphasis of the question. For by and large, it is also not common for most people to privately commission a scribe to write a Torah scroll for them. Indeed, although as quoted above, checking a Torah scroll is considered equivalent to writing one, we do not find most people endeavoring even to check a Torah scroll.

AN ALTERNATE PERSPECTIVE   Rabbeinu Asher interprets the *mitzvah* of writing a Torah scroll in a different manner:[10]

Certainly, it is a great *mitzvah* to write a Torah scroll.... This applies, however, to the earlier generations when they would write Torah scrolls from which to study. At present, when Torah scrolls are written and placed in synagogues for communal reading, the positive *mitzvah* incumbent on all Jewish males who have the capacity, is to write *Chumashim, Mishnayos, Gemaras,* and their commentaries and to ponder upon them.... For [the purpose of] the *mitzvah* of writing the Torah is to study it, as it is written:[2] "...and teach it to the children of Israel, placing it in their mouths."

Through the *Gemara* and its commentaries, one will thoroughly know the interpretation of the *mitzvos* and the [relevant] laws. Therefore, these are the texts that a man is obligated to write.

With regard to the composition of a Torah scroll, by contrast, since the honor of the scroll will be enhanced by it being written by a qualified scribe, there is no preference for a person to write it himself (*T'vuos Shor* 26:14).

10. *Hilchos Ketanos*, the beginning of *Hilchos Sefer Torah*.

This concept is also quoted by the *Shulchan Aruch*.[11] Indeed, there are some authorities[12] who maintain that according to Rabbeinu Asher, in the present age, the *mitzvah* is not to write a Torah scroll, but rather to write "*Chumashim, Mishnayos, Gemoros,* and their commentaries."

On this basis, we can explain the common practice of not seeking to write or commission the writing of a Torah scroll oneself. For in the present age, the scope of the *mitzvah* has been expanded and the *mitzvah* is fulfilled with other texts.

This resolution, however, is not complete, for the common practice is not to write — or print[13] — these other texts, but to purchase them. And the purchase of a Torah scroll is not considered equivalent to writing one. Our Sages[14] equate the purchase of a Torah scroll with "snatching a *mitzvah* from the marketplace." There are some authorities[15] who maintain that one fulfills the *mitz-*

---

11. *Yoreh De'ah. loc. cit.:*2.
12. See the gloss of the *Derisha* to the *Tur (Yoreh De'ah 270).* Note, however, the glosses of the *Beis Yosef* and the *Bayis Chadash* who maintain that even according to Rabbeinu Asher, it is still a *mitzvah* to write a Torah scroll in the present era. See also the commentaries to the *Shulchan Aruch, op. cit.*
13. There is a debate among the *halachic* authorities whether printing is considered equivalent to writing or not. Surely, in the present age, when much of the work in printing is performed by gentiles who cannot, in a *halachic* context, be considered the agents of a Jew, there is a question regarding this matter. (See also the *S'dei Chemed, Pe'as HaSedeh, Klallim, Maareches Dales,* sec. 38, *et al.,* which questions whether texts printed by a gentile can be considered sacred.) These questions are, however, superseded by the fact that the common practice is not to commission the printing of a text oneself, but rather to buy texts that have already been printed.
14. *Menachos* 30a.
15. *Rashi* and the *Nimukei Yosef,* in their commentaries to *Menachos, ibid.* With regard to the *Rambam's* approach, there is a question among the commentaries. For in *Sefer HaMitzvos* (Positive Mitzvah 18), he writes

vah in this manner, but that this is not the desirable manner in which to perform the *mitzvah*. The *Ramah*[16] goes even further and rules that a person who purchases a Torah scroll without checking it "does not fulfill his obligation with it."[17] Therefore, the question arises: Even according to Rabbeinu Asher, how can one fulfill his obligation to write a Torah scroll by purchasing printed texts?

TO WRITE OR TO ACQUIRE? Certain authorities[18] have explained that the difference of opinion between the *Rambam* and Rabbeinu Asher concerns not only the object of the *mitzvah* — a Torah scroll or other Torah texts as well — but also the activity through which the *mitzvah* is fulfilled. According to the *Rambam,* the intent is that each man write a Torah scroll, while according to Rabbeinu Asher, what is important is not the actual writing, but that each person provide himself with Torah texts to study.[19] Thus, by purchasing texts, one would fulfill the *mitzvah*.

The wording Rabbeinu Asher himself uses does not, however, reinforce this conception. For Rabbeinu Asher speaks about a difference in the texts used in his generation and in earlier ones, but nothing more than that. And

---

that if a person purchases a Torah scroll, he fulfills the *mitzvah*. In the *Mishneh Torah,* however, the *Rambam* does not mention the purchase of a Torah scroll at all, leading some to the conclusion that he changed his mind, and does not consider this a means to fulfill the *mitzvah*.

16. *Yoreh De'ah* 270:1.
17. When he checks it, however, it is considered as if he wrote the entire scroll *(Rambam, Mishneh Torah, loc. cit.).*
18. See *Shaagas Aryeh,* sec. 36; *Minchas Chinuch, Mitzvah* 613.
19. This is reflected in the description of the *mitzvah* by *Sefer HaChinuch* *(Mitzvah* 613): "We were commanded that... every Jewish man should have a Torah scroll accessible to him from which to read," i.e., the emphasis is on having a scroll (or texts) available.

he clearly defines the *mitzvah* as "writing *Chumashim...*," not acquiring them.

HOW TO DEFINE THE *MITZVAH*

The difficulty mentioned above can be resolved through the resolution of a fundamental question regarding Rabbeinu Asher's position. If the Torah commands us to write a Torah scroll, how can the object of that *mitzvah* be changed due to circumstance? The Torah and its *mitzvos* are eternal and unchanging.[20] Why then is the definition of a *mitzvah* affected by our changes in study habits?

This question can be resolved by explaining that Rabbeinu Asher considers the *mitzvah* to be defined by its motivating principle.[21]

The verse on which the *mitzvah* is based is: "And now write down this song for yourself, and teach it to the children of Israel, placing it in their mouths." Rabbeinu Asher explains that the intent of the *mitzvah* is to make possible the study of the Torah in a written form. For in this manner, it will be able to be reviewed easily and thus will not be forgotten.[22] And thus, as the passage continues,[23] the Torah will serve as a testimonial for the Jewish people at all times, even in eras when the people "abrogate My covenant."

---

20. See *Rambam, Mishneh Torah, Hilchos Melachim* 11:3; see also the *Rambam's* Thirteen Principles of Faith *(Commentary to the Mishnah, Sanhedrin 10:1),* Principle Nine.
21. See *Chasam Sofer, Yoreh De'ah,* Responsum 254; *Binas Sofer,* 12:1, and others.
22. See the *Jerusalem Talmud, Berachos* 5:1. See also *Shaloh* tractate *Shavuos* (p. 191b); *Sefer HaMaamarim 5701,* p. 17, which states: "Letters make one wise."
23. *Devarim* 31:16ff.

According to this conception, the writing of the scroll *per se* is not the intent of the *mitzvah,* but rather the medium through which the *mitzvah* is fulfilled. At the time when the commandment was given, the only way possible to fulfill the above intent was by writing a Torah scroll — for at that time, it was forbidden to write down the Oral Law.[24] Nevertheless, the *mitzvah* is not to write a Torah scroll, but to enable the Jewish people to study the Torah through written texts.

(To cite a parallel: The Torah commands us to affix a *mezuzah* with the verse:[25] "And you shall write them on the doorposts of your homes...." The scope of this *mitzvah* is not, however, writing the *parshiyos* contained in the *mezuzah,* but rather affixing the *mezuzah* on one's doorposts. Writing is merely one facet of the *mitzvah.*)

Based on this conception, it can be explained that originally, when the only Torah text that one was permitted to write was a Torah scroll, this *mitzvah* could be fulfilled only by writing such a scroll. And while writing such a scroll, one had to adhere to all the provisions appropriate for the holiness of a Torah scroll: e.g., that it be written on parchment that is ruled, that the Assyrian script be used, and that it be written only in Hebrew. When, however, the restriction against writing the Oral Law was rescinded, the *mitzvah* of writing down the Torah was automatically expanded to include other texts. For it is through writing these texts that the intent of the *mitzvah* — the presentation of the Torah as a written testimonial — is fulfilled.

---

24. *Gittin* 60b.
25. *Devarim* 6:9.

JUSTIFICATION FOR RABBEINU ASHER'S POSITION The above concepts are also relevant with regard to the question of whether one can fulfill one's obligation by purchasing a Torah scroll or not. The opinion which maintains that one can fulfill one's obligation by purchasing a Torah scroll maintains that the laws associated with writing a Torah scroll are necessary only to endow a Torah scroll with holiness. If the scroll has already been written in a proper manner, one can fulfill the *mitzvah* of making the scroll available to be studied by purchasing it.

The opinion which does not accept the purchase of a scroll as an acceptable means of observing the *mitzvah,* by contrast, considers all the laws associated with writing a Torah scroll as intrinsic elements of the *mitzvah* itself. Since in that era, the only way the *mitzvah* could be fulfilled was by writing a Torah scroll, and a Torah scroll must be written according to certain specifications, it is only by fulfilling those specifications that one can observe the *mitzvah.*

According to Rabbeinu Asher, however, this would apply only in the previous eras when the *mitzvah* of writing down the Torah involved only the composition of a Torah scroll. In subsequent generations, when the scope of that *mitzvah* was expanded to include other texts which are not governed by these specifications, both approaches would agree that one can fulfill one's obligation by purchasing such texts.

AN UNRESOLVED QUESTION Explanation is nevertheless required. For we do not find our Rabbis advising youth directly upon reaching the age of *Bar Mitzvah* to fulfill this *mitzvah* by purchasing Torah texts. Moreover, as the *Beis Yosef*, the *Bayis Chadash*, and others have explained, Rabbeinu Asher's position should not be interpreted as changing the focus of the *mitzvah* so as not to include the composition of a Torah scroll, but rather as an expansion of its scope, i.e., in addition to the *mitzvah* of writing a Torah scroll, one should *also* provide oneself with *Chumashim, Mishnayos,* and the like.

And thus the original question remains unanswered: Why haven't our Torah Sages throughout the generations sought to fulfill this *mitzvah* by writing Torah scrolls or by having them commissioned? Moreover, even those Sages who did write Torah scrolls did not fulfill the *mitzvah* at the first opportunity which presented itself, but rather later in life.

THE POWER OF THE COMMUNITY The resolution to this question is based on another ruling of the *Rambam*:[26] "The inhabitants of a town should compel each other to build a synagogue and purchase a Torah scroll," i.e., it is common practice for Jewish communities throughout the world to have Torah scrolls written on behalf of the community. In addition to the Torah scrolls which certain individuals have written, and which they endow to the community,[27] the community will commission a Torah scroll to be written, and that

---

26. *Mishneh Torah, Hilchos Tefillah* 11:1; see also a parallel in *Hilchos Shecheinim* 6:1. See the *Tur* and the *Shulchan Aruch (Orach Chayim* 150:1, *Choshen Mishpat* 163:1), and *Shulchan Aruch HaRav, Hilchos Talmud Torah* 4:13.

27. At times, these individuals will give their scrolls to the community as an outright gift, and at times, they will retain ownership over them. See *Pischei Teshuvah, Yoreh De'ah* 270:3.

scroll is the property of the community as a whole.[28] In this manner, every Jew has a share in the *mitzvah* of writing a Torah scroll.

This explanation is nevertheless somewhat problematic: Firstly, there is a question whether a community is considered a single, collective entity or merely an aggregate of individuals.[29] Moreover, even if the community is considered as an aggregate of individuals, our Rabbis write[30] that partners do not fulfill the *mitzvah* of writing a Torah scroll by commissioning the composition of such a scroll, for the *mitzvah* is that each individual write a Torah scroll himself. How then can one fulfill the *mitzvah* through the writing of a communal Torah scroll?

In resolution, it can be explained that in the present age, every person does not have the capacity of writing a Torah scroll himself. Therefore every person fulfills the *mitzvah* with the composition of scrolls by the community.

With regard to partnership, the difficulties raised can be resolved by comparison to the *mitzvah* of *lulav* and *esrog:* A person cannot fulfill his obligation with an *esrog* whose ownership he shares with a partner unless the partner grants him his share as a present,[31] for on the first day, an *esrog* must belong entirely to the person using it for the *mitzvah*.[32] In communities where it is difficult to procure an *esrog,* however, it was customary for the

28. Moreover, as reflected in the laws pertaining to a synagogue, a share in these communal scrolls is not restricted to the people living in the specific community, but also is granted to guests.
29. See *Mefaneach Tzafunos,* ch. 4, sec. 2.
30. See the glosses of Rabbi Akiva Eiger and the *Pischei Teshuvah* to *Yoreh De'ah* 270:1.
31. *Shulchan Aruch, Orach Chayim* 658:7.
32. See *Rashbam, Bava Basra* 137b.

community to buy an *esrog,* and for everyone to use it for the *mitzvah* — even those who did not necessarily know all the *halachic* details of acquiring the *esrog* or granting their share to others.[33]

Why was this acceptable? Since the community purchased the *esrog* so that everyone could use it to fulfill the *mitzvah,* one may assume that everyone gave their share to each person who desired to use the *esrog* to fulfill the *mitzvah,* with the understanding that later that share would be returned to them.

Similarly with regard to the composition of a Torah scroll: Since this is the only way in which most people today can fulfill this *mitzvah,* we can assume that the communal scrolls are being written with the intent that they be considered as belonging to each member of the community individually.

"THE HEART OF THE JEWISH COURT ESTABLISHES THE STIPULATIONS FOR THEM" The above explanation still appears to be somewhat lacking, for the two *mitzvos* are not entirely alike. With regard to an *esrog,* to fulfill the *mitzvah,* it is sufficient to own the *esrog.* With regard to a Torah scroll, by contrast, it is not enough to own the scroll, one must write it — or commission someone else to write it. For this reason, if one inherits a Torah scroll, or according to the *Ramah,* if one purchases a Torah scroll, one does not fulfill the *mitzvah.* Therefore, even if the community grants each person ownership of the scroll, that does not necessarily enable each person to fulfill the *mitzvah* of writing a scroll.

---

33. *Shulchan Aruch, loc. cit.:9.*

This difficulty can be resolved on the basis of the *Talmudic* principle:[34] "The heart of the Jewish court establishes the stipulations for them." It can be explained that when the communal authorities commissioned the writing of a Torah scroll, their intent was not merely that each member of the community would be considered as the owner of the scroll, but that each member of the community would be considered as if he individually commissioned the writing of the scroll and thus could fulfill the *mitzvah* with it.[35]

On this basis, we can understand the importance of the composition of communal Torah scrolls which are written with the specific intent of enabling all Jews to fulfill this *mitzvah*. These scrolls join together all Jews — particularly those who purchased letters in the scrolls — in the performance of this *mitzvah*.

LOOKING TO THE HORIZON The *mitzvah* of writing a Torah scroll was given to the Jewish people — and fulfilled by Moshe *Rabbeinu* — directly before our people's entry into *Eretz Yisrael*. It is the last of the 613 *mitzvos* of the Torah.[36]

---

34. *Kesubbos* 106b. Note the *Sefer HaKobetz* who employs this principle to explain why an individual who donates a Torah scroll which he has had written for himself does not forfeit the *mitzvah* when he donates the scroll to a synagogue for communal use.

35. Moreover, the court commissioning the composition of the Torah scroll need not specify this intent to the scribe; it is sufficient that they have this intent themselves (see *Ritbah, Shavuos* 11a; *Ramah, Orach Chayim* 154:8, *Yoreh De'ah* 259:2).

   Even those who are born after the communal Torah scroll is written have a share in this *mitzvah*. For from time to time, every communal Torah scroll is checked, and by checking and correcting a Torah scroll, one is considered to have fulfilled the *mitzvah*.

36. See *Sefer HaChinuch, Mitzvah* 613.

Our Rabbis have taught[37] us that the fulfillment of this *mitzvah* is one of the preparatory steps leading to the conclusion of the exile and to the advent of the era when we will again enter *Eretz Yisrael,* led by *Mashiach,* and fulfill all the *mitzvos* in the most complete manner. May this take place in the immediate future.

---

37. See *Ben Ish Chai, Derashos, Parshas Bereishis,* p. 7.

GLOSSARY AND
BIOGRAPHICAL INDEX

An asterisk indicates a cross-reference within this Glossary.
All entries are Hebrew unless otherwise indicated.

acharonim (lit., "the later ones"): the Torah sages from the Renaissance period until the present day

Aggadah: the teachings of the *Midrash* and those portions of the *Talmud* which deal with ethics, stories of our Sages, and narratives concerning Biblical figures not included in the Bible

Alshich: Rabbi Moshe Alshich (1521-1593), one of the leading Rabbis of Safed, author of a commentary on the Torah

Amoraim: the sages of the *Gemara*

Anochi (lit., "I am"): the first word of the Ten Commandments which is used as a reference to G-d's essence

areivus: (a) the mutual responsibility that exists among the Jewish people; (b) responsibility as a guarantor

Azazel: a rocky cliff from which a goat — identified with the forces of evil *(Pirkei deRabbi Eliezer,* sec. 46) — was pushed to its death on Yom Kippur *(Vayikra,* ch. 16; *Yoma* 63a).

baal teshuvah (lit., "master of return"; pl., *baalei teshuvah*): a person who turns to G-d in repentance

bar meitzra (Aram.): a neighbor who is granted certain rights with regard to the purchase of adjoining property

bar mitzvah (lit., "one obligated to fulfill the commandments"; Aram./Heb.): the age at which this obligation becomes incumbent on a person, and the celebration marking that occasion

Bayis Chadash (Bach): commentary on the *Tur* by Rabbi Yoel Sirkes (1561-1640)

Beis HaMikdash: the Temple in Jerusalem

Beis Hillel: the School of Hillel

Beis Shammai: the School of Shammai

Beis Yosef: the halachic commentary to the *Tur* written by Rabbi Yosef Karo (1488-1575)

Beraisa (Aram.): a body of teachings authored by Rabbi Yehudah *HaNasi* during the same period as the **Mishnah,* but not included in that text; often quoted in the **Gemara;* when not capitalized, the term refers to a single teaching of this type

bittul: in chassidic terminology, self-nullification, a commitment to G-d and divine service that transcends self-concern; in halachic terminology, the mixture of a minute quantity of a substance with others to the extent that its presence is no longer of consequence

Chagigah: (a) an offering brought to the Temple on the pilgrimage festivals; (b) a tractate of the *Talmud* dealing with such sacrifices

Chanukah (lit., "dedication"): eight-day festival beginning 25 Kislev, commemorating the Maccabees' rededication of the Temple in the second century B.C.E., and marked by the kindling of lights

Chassidus: the body of chassidic thought and philosophy

chazzan: the leader of synagogue services

cheftza (lit., "entity"; Aram.): a term used to imply that the relevant halachic obligations affect it rather than the person involved (**gavra*)

Chessed (lit., "kindness," or "grace"): the Divine attribute which parallels the corresponding human qualities and thus is associated with the dispersion of G-dly light and energy to lower levels of existence

chinuch: education

Chumash: the Five Books of Moses; halachically, such a text as written or printed without adhering to the laws governing the writing of a Torah scroll

din: judgment

derush: the non-literal, homiletic approach to understanding Torah concepts

Eretz Yisrael: the Land of Israel

esrog: a citron, one of the four species of plants used to perform a *mitzvah* on the holiday of Sukkos

gavra (lit., "man"; Aram.): a term used to imply that the *halachic* obligations associated with an entity center on the person performing the action rather than on the entity *(*cheftza)*

Gemara (Aram): the Babylonian *Talmud,* the edition developed in Babylonia, and edited at end of the fifth century C.E.

Geonim (pl. of *gaon*): Torah luminaries; more specifically, the heads of the Babylonian academies after the composition of the *Talmud*

Gevurah (lit., "might"): the Divine attribute which parallels the corresponding human quality and thus is associated with the holding back of Divine revelation and restricting the dispersion of Divine light to lower levels of existence

Haggadah: (lit., "telling"): the text from which the *Seder* service is conducted on the first two nights of Passover in the Diaspora (or on the first night only in Israel)

halachah (adj., halachic): (a) the body of Jewish Law; (b) a single law

Halachos Gedolos: One of the early post-Talmudic halachic texts

Hallel (lit., "praise"): a portion of *Psalms* (113-118) recited in the prayer service on the festivals

Havdalah (lit., "distinction"): the prayer recited at the conclusion of a Sabbath or a festival to distinguish that holy day from the weekdays which follow

Iggeres HaKodesh: the fourth portion of *Tanya,* consisting of a collection of pastoral letters sent by the Alter Rebbe and included in the *Tanya* by his sons

Iggeres HaTeshuvah: the third portion of *Tanya;* a treatise on *teshuvah*

ikkar: of primary importance

ikvesa diMeshicha (Aram.): the last generation before the Redemption, when *Mashiach's* approaching footsteps can be heard

Jerusalem Talmud: the edition of the *Talmud* compiled in *Eretz Yisrael* at end of the fourth century C.E.

Kabbalah (lit., "received tradition"): the Jewish mystical tradition

kares (lit., "excision"): the cutting off of the soul, causing premature death on the earthly plane and a severing of the soul's connection with G-d on the spiritual plane

Kiddush (lit., "sanctification"): blessings recited over a goblet of wine and expressing the sanctity of *Shabbos (e.g., *Siddur,* p. 146) or a festival

kinyan: an act that formalizes a legal transaction

klos hanefesh (lit., "the expiration of the soul"): yearning for closeness to G-d to the extent that the soul actually expires

ko'ach: potential

Kohen: a priest

lemafreia (Aram.): (a) retroactively; (b) out of proper sequence

Likkutei Sichos: the edited collection of the Rebbe's talks

lulav: the palm branch taken during the holiday of *Sukkos

machshirei mitzvah: articles that enable a *mitzvah* to be performed

Maharsha (an acronym for *Moreinu HaRav* Shmuel Eliezer): R. Shmuel Eliezer Eidel's (1555-1631), whose commentary is included in most standard editions of the *Talmud

Malchuyos: one of the blessings of the *Mussaf* service on *Rosh HaShanah, consisting of verses reflecting G-d's Kingship

Mashiach: the Messiah

Megillah (lit., "scroll"): when used as a proper noun without a modifier, it is generally a reference to the Scroll of Esther which relates the narrative commemorated by the holiday of *Purim

mehadrin (Aram.): those who observe the *mitzvos* precisely and lovingly

mehadrin min hamehadrin (Aram.): those whose observance is precise even when compared to the *mehadrin*

Menorah: the seven-branched candelabrum in the Sanctuary

mezuzah: a parchment scroll containing the first two paragraphs of the *Shema* placed at the entrance to homes, and rooms within a home

Midrash: the classic collection of the Sages' homiletical teachings on the Bible

Mishnah (pl., *mishnayos*): the first compilation of the Oral Law authored by Rabbi Yehudah *HaNasi* (approx. 200 C.E.); the germinal statements of law elucidated by the *Gemara,* together with which they constitute the *Talmud; when not capitalized, a single statement of law from this work

Mishneh Torah: the *Rambam's magnum opus,* a compendium of the entire Oral Law

Mitzrayim: Egypt

mitzvah (lit., "commandment"; pl., *mitzvos*): one of the 613 Commandments; in a larger sense, any religious obligation

modeh bemiktzas: one who admits a portion of a claim and is hence obligated by Scriptural Law to take an oath to prove his defense

Nasi (pl., *nesi'im*): (a) in Biblical times, the head of any one of the Twelve Tribes; (b) in later generations, the civil and/or spiritual head of the Jewish community at large

nigleh (lit., "what has been revealed"): the body of Torah law (cf. *pnimiyus haTorah)

nosar: the prohibition against leaving sacrificial meat past the time when it may be eaten

Omer: a Biblical dry measure; an offering of this quantity of barley brought on the day following the first day of Passover; this day and the subsequent forty-eight days are counted in preparation for the holiday of *Shavuos

Or HaChayim: a commentary on the Torah authored by Rabbi Chayim ben Atar of Morocco and later of *Eretz Yisrael* (1696-1743); printed in many editions of the Torah

parshah (pl., *parshiyos,* (lit., "portion"): one of the 54 weekly Torah readings

Pesach: (a) Passover, seven-day festival beginning on 15 Nissan, commemorating the Exodus from Egypt; (b) the sacrifice offered on the eve of that holiday

pnimiyus haTorah (lit., "the inner dimension of the Torah"): the realm of the Torah that deals with mystical truth, hence a synonym for *Chassidus* (cf. *nigleh)

poel: the actual expression of a potential

pshat: the simple explanation of a passage from the Torah or of a Jewish practice

Purim (lit., "lots"): one-day festival falling on 14 Adar and commemorating the miraculous salvation of the Jews of the Persian Empire in the fourth century B.C.E.

Rabbeinu: our teacher, an appellation of respect added to the name of certain great educational leaders

Rabbeinu Nissim (1308-1376): author of a commentary to the *Talmud* and a *halachic* commentary to the work of Rabbeinu Yitzchak Alfasi

Rama (acronym for Rabbi Moshe Isserles; c. 1530-1572): author of the *Mapah,* a *halachic* commentary incorporated into the **Shulchan Aruch* which presents the Ashkenazic halachic perspective

Rambam (acronym for Rabbi Moshe ben Maimon; 1135-1204): Maimonides, one of the foremost Jewish thinkers of the Middle Ages; his **Mishneh Torah* is one of the pillars of Jewish law, and his *Guide to the Perplexed,* one of the classics of Jewish philosophy

Ramban (acronym for Rabbi Moshe ben Nachman (1194-1270): Nachmanides. a sage whose commentaries on the Torah and the *Talmud* are Torah classics

Rashi (acronym for Rabbi Shlomo Yitzchaki; 1040-1105): the author of the foremost commentaries to the Torah and the *Talmud;* leader of the Jewish community in Alsace-Lorraine

Rebbe (lit., "my teacher [or master]"): saintly Torah leader who serves as spiritual guide to a following of chassidim

remez: an allusion, one of the levels of Torah interpretation

reshus (lit., "permitted"): modes of behavior which are neither commanded nor forbidden

revi'is (lit., "a fourth"): a quarter of a *log,* a Talmudic measure often considered the minimum requirement with regard to *mitzvos* and prohibitions that involve drinking

Ritva (acronym for Rabbi Yom Tov ben Avraham, 1248-1330): author of an important Talmudic commentary, a leader of the Spanish Jewish community

Rosh HaShanah (lit., "head of the year"): the solemn New Year festival, falling on 1 and 2 Tishrei

Sanhedrin: (a) the highest Jewish court; (b) the tractate of the *Talmud* of that name

Seder (lit., "order"): the order of service observed at home on the first two nights of Passover

Shabbos (pl., *Shabbosos*): the Sabbath

Shavuos (lit., "weeks"): festival commemorating the Giving of the Torah at Sinai, in *Eretz Yisrael* falling on 6 Sivan, and in the Diaspora on 6-7 Sivan

Sheiltos: a halachic text written by Rav Achai Gaon shortly after the composition of the **Talmud*

Shelah: acronym for *Shnei Luchos HaBris,* a major halachic, ethical and mystical work by Rabbi Yeshayahu Horowitz (c. 1565-1630)

sheliach tzibbur: the leader of communal prayer; the **chazzan*

Shema: the fundamental Jewish prayer which we are obligated to recite every evening and morning

Shemitah: the Sabbatical year

Shemoneh Esreh (lit., "eighteen"): the eighteen blessings instituted to serve as the core of the prayer services recited every morning, afternoon, and evening; also known as the *amidah;* in the **Talmudic* period, a nineteenth blessing was added to these prayers

shevarim: the three **Shofar* blasts of intermediate length

Shofar: the ram's horn sounded on **Rosh HaShanah, and during the month of Elul in preparation for that holiday

Shofaros: one of the blessings of the *Mussaf* service on **Rosh HaShanah, consisting of verses concerning the *Shofar*

Shulchan Aruch (lit., "a set table"): the standard Code of Jewish Law compiled by R. Yosef Caro in the mid-sixteenth century; also used to refer to later codes; e.g., the *Shulchan Aruch HaRav* compiled by R. Shneur Zalman of Liadi

Shulchan Aruch HaRav: the Code of Jewish Law compiled by the Alter Rebbe

sichah (pl., *sichos*): an informal Torah talk delivered by a Rebbe

sod: the mystical dimension of Torah study

sotah: (a) a woman suspected of immodest conduct whose fidelity is put to the test; see *Numbers,* ch. 5; (b) a Talmudic tractate of that name

sukkah (lit., "booth"; pl., *sukkos*): a temporary dwelling in which we are commanded to live during the festival of *Sukkos

Sukkos (lit., "Booths"): seven-day festival (eight days in the Diaspora) beginning on 15 Tishrei, taking its name from the temporary dwelling in which one lives during this period

tafel (lit., "of secondary importance"): an object which is subordinate to another object described as *ikkar

Talmud: the basic compendium of Jewish law, thought, and Biblical commentary, comprising *Mishnah and *Gemara; when unspecified refers to the Babylonian *Talmud,* the edition developed in Babylonia, and edited at end of the fifth century C.E.; the *Jerusalem Talmud* is the edition compiled in *Eretz Yisrael at end of the fourth century C.E.

Tanach: the Bible

Tanna: a sage of the *Mishnah

Tanya: the classic text of Chabad chassidic thought authored by the Alter Rebbe

tekiah (pl., *tekios*): the protracted *Shofar blast

teruah (pl., *teruos*): the short staccato *Shofar blast

teshuvah (lit., "return [to G-d]"): repentance

Tosafos (lit., "supplements"): classical commentaries on the *Talmud beginning to appear in the mid-twelfth century

Tosefta (Aram. "supplement"): a body of teachings authored during the same period as the *Mishnah,* but not included in that text; when not capitalized, the term refers to a single teaching of this type

Turei Zahav: a commentary on the *Shulchan Aruch written by R. David Halevi (1586-1667), printed together with most editions of the *Shulchan Aruch

tzaddik (pl., *tzaddikim*): righteous man

tzedakah: charity

tzitzis: the fringes worn at the corners of four-cornered garments *utzericha:* a Talmudic technique of exposition in which the need for seemingly redundant phrases or teachings is elucidated

yeshivah (pl., *yeshivos*): Torah academy for advanced students

yetzer hara: the evil inclination

Yirmeyahu: the prophet Jeremiah

Yom Kippur: the Day of Atonement, fast day falling on 10 Tishrei and climaxing the Days of Awe

Yom-Tov: festival

Yovel: the Jubilee year

Zohar (lit., "radiance"): the classic text of the **Kabbalah*